Dictionary of L A W

Dictionary of
LAW

George Gordon Coughlin

BARNES & NOBLE BOOKS
A DIVISION OF HARPER & ROW, PUBLISHERS
New York, Cambridge, Philadelphia,
San Francisco, London, Mexico City, São Paulo, Sydney

FIRST EDITION

Designed by Sidney Feinberg

Library of Congress Cataloging in Publication Data

Coughlin, George Gordon.
  Dictionary of law.
  "EH/539."
  1. Law—United States—Dictionaries.   I. Title.

| KF156.C68 | 349.73′03′21 | 81-47079 |
| ISBN 0-06-463539-2 (pbk.) | 347.300321 | AACR2 |

---

82 83 84 85 86 10 9 8 7 6 5 4 3 2 1

Preface

This book is not intended for lawyers, but as a quick reference tool in which lay people can find the meanings of legal words and phrases that may affect or relate to their everyday lives.

I practiced law for over 50 years, and like other experienced lawyers, I know the basic meaning of common legal words and phrases from practice and training. In preparing this book, however, to make sure that I was right I consulted encyclopedias of law such as *Corpus Juris Secundum (C.J.S.)*, published by the American Law Book Company; *Black's Law Dictionary*, published by West Publishing Company; and *Ballantine's Law Dictionary*, published by the Lawyers Co-operative Publishing Company.

The above-mentioned works are scholarly and exhaustive. But in my own treatment of legal words and phrases, I selected terms I considered useful or interesting to general readers, and tried to define them clearly and concisely, with a number of examples to show how they apply in actual situations. For example, there are many legal maxims, in Latin and in English. I cover only a few maxims, those which are commonly used.

Many words and phrases have commonly accepted popular meanings and also related legal meanings. There are some words that have popular meanings and may also be used in unrelated legal senses, such as the following:

Word	Popular meaning	Legal meaning
Action	Conduct or doing something	Lawsuit or legal proceeding in court
Suit	Article of clothing	Lawsuit
Exhibit	Something shown or displayed at an exhibition	Paper or article produced and identified in a court proceeding
Information	Knowledge or news	Formal accusation of a crime
Motion	Movement	Application for a court order

This book gives the legal meaning of these terms. SMALL CAPITALS are used for cross-reference.

Don't forget, if you want an explanation or data in depth or detail, go to the previously cited encyclopedia or law dictionaries. My explanations are simplified to make them understandable. It is my hope that the reader will gain from them not only a general knowledge of legal terminology, but also some understanding of the legal principles that undergird our government and society.

This book should be used as a reference book the same as any other specialized dictionary. In no event should it be used to replace a lawyer, who should be consulted whenever you have a legal problem. Someone once said that a person who acts as his own attorney has a fool for a client. Don't make the mistake of trying to solve your own legal problems.

Dictionary of L A W

A

abandonment. The voluntary giving up of property without turning over the ownership to some other person. Abandonment is in effect a surrender of a right to property. Whether or not there has been an abandonment of property may be most important in legal cases. Abandonment is to be distinguished from other means of parting with ownership of property, such as (a) sale or transfer of property, (b) gift of property, (c) loss of property, (d) neglect to maintain property, (e) estoppel (which is inconsistent with claim of ownership).

Abandonment depends on intention to relinquish ownership of property. This intention may be expressed (orally or in writing) or implied.

Abandonment generally is applicable to personal property, not real estate. Of course, as a practical matter real estate may be abandoned if the owner does not pay taxes on the property and the government sells it for taxes.

Example of abandonment of personal property: John Brown decides he no longer has any use for a gas stove which he owns. So he gets the assistance of a neighbor to move the stove to an alley back of his house. Items left in the alley are generally picked up by scavengers or people who look for something for nothing. There has been an abandonment of the stove when John Brown causes it to be put in the alley. .

abatement. A reduction or lessening. Among the various items in law that may be *abated* are taxes (which may be reduced or refunded) and lega-

1

cies in an estate where there are insufficient assets to pay the legacies in full.

abduction. The taking away or KIDNAPPING of a person by force. Often the word abduction is used to denote the taking of a female by force to effect a marriage or for prostitution.

abortion. The use of artificial means to bring about the miscarriage, expulsion, or destruction of a human fetus.

The United States Supreme Court has held that a woman has the right, in consultation with her physician, to have an abortion performed during the first trimester (three-month period) of her pregnancy. After the first trimester, state legislation may regulate abortions to protect the woman's health during the second trimester and to protect the fetus during the final trimester.

abstracts of title. A summary statement of documents or facts which affect the ownership of REAL ESTATE. Commonly referred to as "abstracts," they are used to determine whether the owner of real estate has a CLEAR TITLE to the real estate.

The purpose of an abstract of title is to present the history of ownership of the land in question, so that a person examining the abstract may ascertain the validity of the title of real estate without actually examining the official records themselves, or, if there is some question as to what the records show, may facilitate examination of those records.

The mere fact that John Jones has an abstract covering his land does not mean that Jones owns the land in question. All that the abstract means is that an *abstractor* has searched the indices of public records and found only the INSTRUMENTS set forth in the abstract.

In the history of the title to a particular parcel of real estate, each DEED or other means of conveyance is a link in the CHAIN OF TITLE. Abstracts of title used to be made only by public officials (such as county clerks). Today they are mostly made by private individuals or companies.

The abstract should contain all relevant information affecting the title of the property in question, such as deeds, wills, encumbrances, liens, and discharges of those encumbrances and liens.

Example: John Smith wants to sell his house. He has no abstract. He goes to a lawyer who specializes in real estate matters. The lawyer tells Smith that he will have to have an abstract to show that he owns the house. The lawyer goes to the courthouse and searches the public records for a period of years (perhaps 40 or 50), beginning with the time when a man by the name of Jones gave a warranty deed to A. The abstract contains a copy of the deed from Jones to A, a copy of deeds from A to B, from B to C, the transcript of records of the probate court of the estate of C, a copy of the deed from the heirs of C to D, a copy of the deed from D to Smith, etc.

abuse of discretion. In law, any public officials and judicial officers are given wide DISCRETION in acting or making DETERMINATIONS. If the action or determination is unreasonable, capricious, or arbitrary, the law says that such action or determination was an abuse of discretion.

> *Example:* John Jones sued Howard Smith. Smith felt that he couldn't get a fair trial in Tompkins County, where the case was sued, because of prejudice on the part of residents of Tompkins County against Smith, and he made a motion for a CHANGE OF VENUE, or place of trial. The motion was heard before Judge McDonald, who didn't like Smith. The matter of change of venue normally is a matter to be decided within the discretion of the trial judge, Judge McDonald. Judge McDonald denied the motion for a new trial. On appeal, the high court held that there was an abuse of discretion on the part of Judge McDonald in denying the motion.

abuse of process. The means by which a civil or criminal proceeding is instituted is called a PROCESS. If process is used for some personal, malicious, or spiteful objective and contrary to the purpose for which the process was intended, that use is called an abuse of process.

acceleration clause. The provision in a contract or written document that upon the happening of a certain event, certain rights will accrue or the entire amount of a debt will become due and payable.

> *Example:* A mortgage may contain a provision that upon the failure of the owner of the mortgaged property to pay taxes, the entire amount of the mortgage would become due and payable. Such a clause in the mortgage is an acceleration clause.

accessory. Although this word may be used in civil or criminal matters, it is most frequently used in criminal matters to mean a person who aids or contributes to the commission of a CRIME. See PARTICEPS CRIMINIS.

accident. In popular usage, something unexpected. In the legal sense the term is generally used when there is a question of whether or not a person or thing has suffered an accident. For example, why is a person disabled—from natural causes such as disease, or because of an accident?

In law an accident is generally considered to be opposite to something planned or intended. Most often accidents with which the law deals arise from human fault or NEGLIGENCE. Sometimes in the law of negligence, if it is difficult to blame the accident on someone's fault or negligence, the accident is said to be unavoidable: that is, it could not have been prevented by reasonable care or prudence.

Example of unavoidable accident: John Smith was driving his car in a normal way. Suddenly the left front wheel came loose and fell off, causing the car to career across the highway and strike the automobile of Thomas Brown. Smith had no warning that the wheel was loose or would become disengaged from the car. The accident and the damage to Brown were unavoidable, and Smith was held blameless. (Perhaps the mechanic who repaired the car shortly before the accident was legally to blame.)

accord and satisfaction. A fancy name for a legal settlement. Technically, the accord is the agreement to settle, and SATISFACTION is the carrying out of the SETTLEMENT.

In order for there to be an accord and satisfaction, there must be a controversy or dispute (e.g. as to the amount owing, one person's liability to another, or the ownership of property). Generally accord and satisfaction takes place when two or more parties agree as to the settlement of a disputed claim. The dispute may arise out of an alleged BREACH OF CONTRACT or from some act or failure to act. (See TORT.) It is not necessary that an accord and satisfaction be put in writing. Compare COMPROMISE AND SETTLEMENT.

Example: Robert Smith and William Jones have an automobile accident that results in a bent fender on Jones' car. Smith and Jones make some measurements and decide that Smith's car was over the center line of the highway and on the wrong side of the road. Neither wants to file a formal insurance claim since the damage is minor, so they decide to make a settlement on the spot. Smith agrees to pay Jones the sum of $65.00 to cover the cost of repair to Jones' fender. The amount is satisfactory to Jones. The next day Smith brings Jones a check for $65.00 and Jones gives Smith a receipt "in full settlement." The parties have made an accord and satisfaction.

account stated. Whenever a debtor and a creditor have a running account, there may come a time when the parties agree that the balance owed by the debtor to the creditor is a certain amount; this is generally called an account stated.

Example: John Doe runs a wholesale grocery. Richard Roe owns a retail grocery store. Doe sells Roe $10,000 worth of merchandise. Roe makes 24 payments to Doe, aggregating $7,000. One day Roe says to Doe, "I am getting behind financially. Things are getting worse. As of March 1, I owe you $3,000." Doe agrees that $3,000 is the balance. Roe says, "I am going to sell what's on my shelves. Then I think I'll be able to pay you," but Doe is not satisfied and sues for faster payment. Instead of recounting the story of all the merchandise Doe sold Roe and of the various amounts paid by Roe to Doe,

Doe simply says in his court papers that on or about March 1 an account was stated between the parties whereby it was agreed that Roe owed Doe $3,000.

accounting. The recording of business and financial transactions. For hundreds of years the law has required certain people to account for money or property. The English common law provided for "action for account," which required anyone who received money or property for the account of another person to file an accounting, showing what happened to the money or property and what, if anything, was left. Today, anyone in a FIDUCIARY position may be required by the court to file an accounting.

PROBATE courts have special machinery to require executors, administrators, trustees, guardians, and other fiduciary persons to file accountings. Although we tend to think of fiduciaries as executors or administrators, there are many persons in other relationships (such as that of agent or partner) who are fiduciaries, and the courts may require such fiduciaries to file accountings. Fiduciaries may be required to account not only for the money or property entrusted to them, but for all commissions or profits received from the money or property.

acknowledgment. A statement made before a notary public, commissioner of deeds, or other officer, asserting that a certain legal instrument (such as a deed) is the act of the person signing it. An acknowledgment is often confused with a JURAT or VERIFICATION. I have known many persons who have executed legal documents and who, when they are brought before or introduced to a notary public say, "I swear." That is wrong. They should say, "I acknowledge that I have executed this document." Generally an acknowledgment is necessary so that the document may be recorded in a public office or received as evidence in a court of law. Acknowledgment may refer to the act of having the instrument itself executed before a proper officer, such as a notary public or commissioner of deeds, or it may refer to the certificate or other evidence of the act of acknowledgment.

An acknowledgment is necessary when the law states that the particular kind of instrument must be acknowledged so that it can be recorded in a public office. An unacknowledged instrument between parties is valid.

Example: John Brown sells James Smith a vacant lot. Smith pays Brown the money for the lot. Brown signs and gives Smith a deed. No notary is present to take Brown's acknowledgment. The deed is good between Brown and Smith, but Smith will have some difficulty having the deed recorded in the county clerk's office.

acquittal. This term may be applied to both criminal and civil law, but most frequently it is used in criminal law to mean a DISCHARGE or RELEASE from criminal liability and to indicate that the person who had been accused is innocent.

Act of God. A happening due to natural causes and not caused by any human agency. An Act of God (sometimes referred to by the French phrase FORCE MAJEURE) may be an accident or a disaster; the implication is that it was brought about by nature and not man. Acts of God enter into the law of negligence. When a person is charged with negligence or lack of care, he may show that the injury was caused not by human negligence but solely by an Act of God. Forces of nature that may amount to Acts of God include storms, fires caused by lightning, violent winds, perils of the sea, tornadoes, hurricanes, unexpected freezes, and landslides.

> *Example.* John Jones had a small farm completely fenced in. During a bad storm, lightning struck a tree on the farm, causing it to fall on and smash a fence. Immediately Jones' cattle walked through a hole in the broken fence and wandered out onto the nearby highway, endangering motorists. Jones' lawyer successfully defended Jones in court on the grounds that the escape of the cattle was caused by an Act of God.

action. A lawsuit in a court of justice whereby one or more plaintiffs sue one or more defendants for the enforcement of a legal right or the redress of a legal wrong. Sometimes "action" is synonymous with "proceeding," but in some states the legislature defines the difference between an action and a proceeding. Basically an action is a lawsuit instituted by one person or corporation against another. In some states the term PROCEEDING has a broader meaning than action, and may refer to any procedure litigants take, with or without a lawsuit, to bring their GRIEVANCES before a tribunal of justice.

> *Example of an action:* Mary Brown borrows $300 from Richard Smith, agreeing to pay that sum to Smith in 6 months with interest at 7%. She does not pay in 6 months. So Smith goes to a lawyer, saying, "I want to sue Mary Brown for $300 plus interest." The lawyer prepares a SUMMONS and COMPLAINT, detailing the facts about the loan and Brown's failure to pay. The lawyer SERVES the summons and complaint on Brown. The complaint demands JUDGMENT for $300 and interest. Richard Smith has started an action against Mary Brown.

Actions are grouped into various classifications. *Actions at law* ask for legal relief. *Actions in equity* ask for equitable relief. *Actions ex contractu* arise out of a CONTRACT. *Actions in rem* are actions against a thing rather than against the person.

Example of an action **in rem:** Richard Roe lends John Doe a piano. John Doe does not return the piano. Roe brings an action against Doe, requiring the sheriff to REPLEVY or seize the piano. Roe has started an action *in rem.*

adjective law. See SUBSTANTIVE LAW.

administrative law. A body of law, developed during the last 50 years, concerned principally with government agencies other than courts or legislatures. A government agency is generally created by a provision in a state constitution or by the legislature.

Some states have Administrative Procedure Acts, which govern administrative agencies such as workmen's compensation boards, the public service commissions, the state boards of medical examiners, etc. Administrative procedure acts prescribe how government agencies shall adopt rules and regulations and make those rules available to the public for inspection. Government agencies must provide opportunity to various interested groups to submit their views with respect to proposed rules and regulations. Agencies must also provide for the filing and publication of the rules and regulations when they are adopted. Administrative procedure acts provide for JUDICIAL REVIEW of PROCEEDINGS by administrative agencies. Such reviews are called CERTIORARI proceedings.

administrator. See EXECUTORS AND ADMINISTRATORS.

admiralty law. Admiralty or maritime law deals with events or subject matter relative to navigable waters. Article 3, section 2 of the United States Constitution says, "The judicial power shall extend . . . to all cases of admiralty and maritime jurisdiction."

Admiralty law is not restricted to the high seas, but extends to all NAVIGABLE WATERS used for commerce. Even canals have been held to be navigable waters and subject to admiralty jurisdiction.

Example of admiralty jurisdiction: A huge freighter carrying iron ore from Duluth, Minnesota, to the city of Buffalo collided with another freighter on Lake Michigan. The determination of blame for the accident was decided by the Admiralty Court in the City of Detroit.

Admiralty law has a unique jargon, such as *libel* (meaning seizure), *charter party* (meaning contract to lease a ship), *prizes* (vessels taken by wartime power), and *arrest of property* (also meaning seizure).

In admiralty courts the trial of an action takes place before a federal judge without a jury.

Seamen are regarded as wards of the admiralty courts, and any legislation regarding seamen is usually construed in their favor.

admissible evidence. A judge or a jury should base any decision upon legal

EVIDENCE. The courts and legislatures of the various states and the federal government have laid down rules to determine what evidence is appropriate and proper to help a judge or jury determine the truth of a matter in issue. If the evidence is received under those rules, it is admissible; otherwise it should be rejected.

Example: John Jones sues Herbert Smith for injuries received when Smith drove his automobile into an automobile driven by Jones. Jones' lawyer tried to prove that Smith had an accident with another car one week before the Jones accident. Evidence of the other accident was IMMATERIAL and INADMISSIBLE, because it didn't concern the accident in question. In order for any evidence to be admissible, it must relate to the subject matter of the lawsuit.

adoption of persons. The establishment of a legal relationship of parent and child between persons who are not so related by BLOOD. Legal adoption is regulated by the individual states. Therefore one must look to the law of each state to find out the requirements for adoption in that state.

Consent of the various parties is a necessary ingredient of the adoption procedure. Among those parties whose consent is generally required are the adopting parents, the natural mother of an illegitimate child (in some cases courts have ruled that unmarried fathers too must be consulted), natural parents, the public placement agency, and depending on age, the person to be adopted. Adoption is generally effected through a judicial procedure authorized by the legislature.

What is the effect of adoption on the parties involved? Most states provide that adopted children have the same rights as natural children with reference to support, custody, earnings, and inheritance.

adultery. Voluntary sexual intercourse by a married person with someone other than the offender's husband or wife. It is to be distinguished from fornication, incest, rape, or seduction. Adultery is a crime in some states but it is rarely prosecuted.

adverse party. The PARTY on the other side of a lawsuit.

Example: John Smith witnessed an accident. One of the parties to the lawsuit interviews Smith and takes a statement from him, but does not call him as a witness. The other side of the lawsuit decides to use Smith as a witness. Hence he is subpoenaed and called as a witness for the adverse party.

adverse possession. The holding of property to which legal TITLE is claimed by another party. Adverse possession may apply to certain items of personal property, but generally it applies to real estate.

Legal title may be acquired by adverse possession where the possession is open, notorious, and hostile (unfriendly or unneighborly) under a claim of title and the possession continues for a certain length of time. In other words, the possossion of an *adverse claimant* must be so open that the true owner is bound to know that the adverse claimant is occupying the land. The possession should be conspicuous and notorious, so that such possession is generally known in the neighborhood.

Another requirement is that the possession be exclusive. This means that where title is in dispute by several people, one and one alone must have adverse possession of the land to the exclusion of all others. Still another requirement is hostility toward the person who has the legal title.

A final requirement of adverse possession in most states is that possession must be continuous for the full statutory period. Mere sporadic possession is not sufficient. For how long a period of time must adverse possession exist before the title to the land is acquired? The answer varies widely from state to state. Some states require possession for 5 years, other states 7 years; some states have a duration requirement of 15 years, others, 20 years; and so it goes.

You may say these requirements for adverse possession are severe, but after all, the adverse claiment is trying to get title to land he doesn't own. In fact, adverse possession has been called "title by thievery."

affiant. A person who makes and signs an AFFIDAVIT.

affidavit. A written, signed, and sworn statement. An affidavit is to be distinguished from sworn TESTIMONY or a DEPOSITION. In the case of sworn testimony or a deposition, notice is given to the ADVERSE PARTY and an opportunity is given for CROSS-EXAMINATION of the person who gives the testimony. But this is not so in the case of an affidavit.

Very often the officer (e.g., a NOTARY PUBLIC) taking the oath has a seal which he affixes, but except in special circumstances the seal is not necessary.

When affidavits are taken in foreign jurisdictions, there must be some authentication by a public officer (such as a clerk of a court) to prove that the official taking the sworn statement had authority to act.

Example of an affidavit: State of New York
                                                         City of Syracuse

Frank White, being duly sworn, deposes and says:

I was standing on the northwest corner of Oak and Butternut Streets in the city of Syracuse, on March 2, 1982, about 3 P.M., when I saw an automobile accident. Oak Street at that point is a through street. A blue Cadillac automobile was being driven north on Oak Street. A yellow Volkswagen was being driven east on Butternut Street. Butternut Street at that point has a stop sign. The Volkswagen did not stop for the stop sign and ran into the right front end of the Cadillac. Before the accident I did not know either of the parties, and I have no interest in the matter.

(signed) _____

Frank White

Subscribed to and sworn to before me this 10th day of March, 1982.

_____

Harold Brown, Notary Public
Onondaga County, New York

affirm. To approve, ratify, or confirm. **1.** The approval by an appellate court of a lower court decision. **2.** To attest to the truth of a written or spoken declaration without taking an oath or appealing to the deity as in the case of swearing before God. See SWEAR.

against the weight of evidence. If the decision of a court or the verdict of a jury is contrary to the credible evidence at the trial, a motion for a new trial may be based on the fact that the verdict was against the weight of evidence.

agent. A person who acts for or REPRESENTS another. The person for whom the agent acts or whom he or she represents is called the *principal.*

The law of agency is a very important branch of law, so fundamental that it affects everyone's life, almost daily.

Though this fact is not emphasized in the world's marketplaces, most agents have FIDUCIARY relationships to their principals. That means the agent owes certain obligations to his principal: to keep his principal advised as to all important facts; not to acquire any interests adverse to those of his principal; not to act as agent for his principal and for another party in the same transaction; not to engage in a rival business; to carry out meticulously all instructions of his principal; to account regularly for all monies of his principal coming into his hands; and not to make any personal profit from a matter relating to the agency without the consent of his principal.

Sometimes there is doubt as to whether or not an agent has the authority to act for an alleged principal. If the principal confirms and accepts the benefits of what the agent does, the authority of the agent is ratified just as though the agent originally had been given authority by the principal. An agent's authority may be *expressed, implied,* or *apparent.*

aggravated assault, See ASSAULT.

alien. A person who owes allegiance to a foreign country of which he is a citizen or subject. Aliens may be residents or nonresidents of the United States. How long they may continue to be residents depends on the provisions of the immigration laws. In order to remain, aliens owe temporary allegiance to the United States and must conform to its laws.

In many respects, the rights and obligations of an alien are the same as those of a citizen. An alien may sue and be sued just the same as a citizen. An alien has the benefit of many U.S. constitutional protections such as freedom of speech, freedom of religion, etc. An alien may obtain permission to work at a trade or occupation just as a citizen does.

The federal government requires aliens to register periodically while they are in the United States. Federal laws treat aliens liberally, but individual states may pass laws preventing aliens from buying real estate. (Such state control of the purchase of real estate by aliens is significant today, because in some states the purchase of real estate by aliens is becoming an increasingly large percentage of all such purchases.)

An alien applying for U.S. citizenship must have an understanding of the English language and a knowledge of American history and government. In most American cities there are civic organizations as well as public education classes that teach English, history, and government to aliens who wish to become citizens. An alien must be considered of good moral character in order to become a citizen, and must have lived in the United States for at least five years. Finally, the candidate for citizenship must take an oath of allegiance to the United States.

alienation of affections. An interference with the marital relationship by a third person, who may or may not be a relative.

alimony. The amount awarded by the court for a husband (as a general rule) to pay his wife or former wife for her support either during the pendency of a DIVORCE or SEPARATION suit or as a final determination in the divorce or separation suit. Alimony may be either temporary or permanent. In some states, provisions have now been made for wives to pay alimony to their husbands in certain circumstances.

allegation. An assertion in a legal pleading that a certain fact is true. The ADVERSE PARTY to a lawsuit may admit or deny the allegation. Only at the trial of the case in court will it be determined whether or not the allegation is true.

amicus curiae. A Latin expression meaning "friend of the court." A person who wishes to appear as an *amicus* or file an *amicus brief* must have the court's permission.

Theoretically the function of an *amicus curiae* is to aid or assist the court, but as a practical matter he is authorized to appear or file a brief in a case whose outcome concerns him because he has a similar or related problem. The theory of allowing an *amicus* to take a positive stand before the court is that the question presented is of general or public interest.

Example: I once attended a 10-day course on taxation conducted by New York University. It was called the Institute of Federal Taxation. The 10 days I spent in New York cost me about $800, which I took as a deduction on my federal income tax return. Internal Revenue disallowed the deduction, saying it was "educational," not professional expense. I took the case to the Tax Court, which beat me. I appealed to the Court of Appeals. The American Medical Association was interested in the outcome of the case because doctors constantly attend educational seminars similar to the one I attended. The A.M.A. asked for and received permission to file a brief, as *amicus curiae.* I won the appeal. (The case is known as *Coughlin* v. *the Commissioner.*)

animals, law of. Law generally is a set of rules for the conduct of human beings. So what has that got to do with animals? The answer is that mankind has interwoven his civilization so closely with animals that there are bound to be legal problems related to them. Animals owned by individuals are a form of property, and law is closely connected with any form of property.

State governments have the power to regulate ownership of animals, to license dogs and cats, and to regulate and inspect the branding or marketing of cattle, horses, and other animals.

Animals get diseases. Both the federal and state governments have the power to inspect, test, cure, and prevent the spreading of disease in both domestic and wild animals. The last-mentioned right may necessitate destruction of the animal, in which case compensation may be paid to the owner.

Humanity seeks to protect dumb animals from human cruelties, and legislatures have passed laws forbidding wanton abuse, beating, or killing of animals. The courts have upheld such laws.

When is an owner of an animal liable for its causing an injury to another person? Animals, broadly speaking, are divided into two classes, wild and domestic. The owner of a wild animal is liable for injuries caused by the animal, even though the animal is partially domesticated.

Example of liability of owner of a wild animal: Joe Jones owns a pet raccoon. Daily the raccoon is allowed to play in Jones' yard. A neighbor's 3-year-old child goes to Jones' yard and plays with the raccoon, receiving scratches and serious injuries to his eyes. Jones is liable for those injuries.

An owner is not liable for injuries inflicted by a domestic animal such as a dog unless the owner has previous knowledge (known in law as SCIENTER) of the vicious propensity of the animal.

> *Example of nonliability of the owner of a domestic animal:* Bob Smith has a 3-year-old Airedale dog known as Scott. Smith took Scott calling on his friend George Jones, who has a 10-year-old son named Harold. Scott and Harold went outdoors to play. Harold apparently teased Scott and Scott attacked Harold, biting his arms and legs. This was the first time that anyone had ever heard of Scott's biting a human being. A jury returned a verdict in favor of Smith, holding that Smith had no *scienter* of Scott's vicious propensity.

There is an old saying that "every dog is entitled to one bite." That is an inaccurate way of attempting to illustrate the rule that an owner must have knowledge of the dog's biting propensity in order to be liable.

annuity. See INSURANCE.

annulment. As used in matrimonial law, the dissolution of the bonds of matrimony on the ground that the marriage was VOID from the beginning. Some persons prefer an annulment to divorce for religious reasons. An annulled marriage is regarded in law and religion as never having taken place.

appeal and error. Judicial machinery for REVIEW by appellate courts of decisions of lower courts. This is in effect an admission by judicial authorities that there is always the possibility of ERROR creeping into the judicial system. Try though we may to achieve perfection, human error is bound to be found in our courts. To protect litigants from such human error, they are given the opportunity to have higher courts review the decisions of the courts below to determine that the original judgments are free from error.

The person who takes an appeal to an appellate court is called the *appellant* or the *plaintiff in error*. The person against whom the appeal is taken is called the *appellee, respondent,* or the *defendant in error*.

An *error of law* is a mistaken ruling of law by the judge who presided in the court trial of the case. An *error of fact* may be a wrong decision made by the jury or the court that made the decision that is the basis of the judgment from which an appeal is taken. In the case of a jury's verdict, the appellant may claim that the verdict is contrary to the facts or is overwhelmingly AGAINST THE WEIGHT OF EVIDENCE produced in court. Rulings on questions of law may concern the admission of evidence; constitutional issues; the validity of a real estate title, a statute or ordinance, or a franchise; the excessiveness or inadequacy of the amount of damages awarded; the custody of children; contracts; marital matters; the right to hold public office; injunctions; zoning districts; property valuations; charges of law to the jury; and criminal matters in general.

Sometimes a person who appeals to an appellate court raises a new point as the basis for review and overturning of the decision of the court below. But generally raising a new point on appeal is too late; the appellant should have raised the question in the court below. If a litigant's lawyer fails to object to the admission of evidence during the trial of the action, he cannot urge an appellate court to rule that the evidence was improperly admitted.

appearance. This word is a good example of how a legal meaning may be entirely different from an ordinary meaning. Ordinary use of this word means the act of showing up. Legally, an appearance means submitting oneself to a court's jurisdiction.

Appearance in a court action is made in a number of ways, including filing a notice of appearance, making an entry on the court's docket, filing a bond, putting up bail, filing a defensive plea, and filing a waiver of service of process.

An appearance may be general or special. A *general appearance* is one in which a party submits to a court's jurisdiction for all purposes; a *special appearance* is one made for the purpose of raising an objection to the jurisdiction of the court.

appellant. See APPEAL AND ERROR.

appellate court. See COURT and APPEAL AND ERROR.

arbitration. A proceeding in which a single person or several persons hears and settles a dispute. The business world is inclined to like arbitration because it eliminates the delays and red tape of court proceedings. Most states have statutes that govern arbitration and make arbitration awards just as binding as court judgments. Thirty-five states have adopted the Uniform Arbitration Act or laws substantially similar.

Submissions to arbitration should (a) be in writing; (b) give the names of the parties to the dispute; (c) explain what the controversy is all about; (d) give the names of the arbitrator or arbitrators; (e) fix the time and place of the hearing; and (f) contain an agreement of the parties to be bound by whatever award is made. Parties may pick their own arbitrators. Or, if they can't find arbitrators acceptable to both sides, they may call on the American Arbitration Association for suggested names of people who are willing to act as arbitrators.

arraignment. The first step after a person is accused by a GRAND JURY INDICTMENT. At the arraignment, the individual has the indictment read to him, is advised as to his constitutional rights, and is asked whether he pleads guilty or not guilty to the charge.

arrest. The detention or seizing of a person suspected of a crime. For an arrest to be valid it must be made by a person having legal authority and with the intent to deprive the accused of liberty until the determination of his innocence or guilt.

arson. The intentional and malicious burning of property. Originally the crime of arson was limited to dwelling houses, but states have now extended the definition to the burning of buildings generally. Also, a number of states have made it a crime to set fire to forest lands.

articles of incorporation. The written document (sometimes called a CHARTER) that creates a private CORPORATION.

assault and battery. Assault and battery is comprised of two parts: (a) assault (a threat of violence or personal injury) and (b) battery (follow-up by the use of violence). The term has two aspects: criminal and civil.

An assault and battery is a crime. Criminal statutes theoretically distinguish between an assault and a battery, but as a practical matter in nine out of ten cases a person is arrested not just for an assault or a battery, but for an assault and battery. Technically again (the law is full of technicalities), a battery does not have to be as forceful as a beating. Mere touching may constitute a battery if it results in an injury.

Also bear in mind that an assault technically may be committed by a mere threat of violence or injury, provided the person committing the assault has the means of carrying out his threat. The assault must be a show of force such as a display of a deadly weapon or the display of such force as to frighten the other person. The person who brings suit must show that the assaulter had the means to carry out the threat.

The battery part of assault and battery may result in lawsuits to establish civil LIABILITY for the injury.

There are a number of defenses to a charge of assault and battery, including accident, self-defense, defense of another person, reasonable defense of property, and eviction of a trespasser from property.

An assault that results in serious bodily injury, that is vicious in nature, or that involves the use of a deadly weapon is called an *aggravated assault*.

assignment. Transfer of ownership. All kinds of property, tangible and intangible, can be the subject of an assignment. Custom has caused certain types of assignments to be made by written INSTRUMENTS bearing particular labels. Among them are the following:

Kind of property	Label for instrument of assignment
Real estate	Deed
Article of personal property	Bill of sale
Mortgage	Assignment
Bill of exchange, check, or note	Indorsement
Money-due account	Assignment
Lease, contract, cause of action, security for debt, interest in an estate, wages, proceeds, judgment, etc.	Assignment

assignment for the benefit of creditors. The United States Constitution gives Congress the right to make laws governing BANKRUPTCY, which is thus subject to the control of the federal government. (See BANKRUPTCY LAWS.) But hundreds of years ago the old English COMMON LAW had a proceeding called assignment for the benefit of creditors. The American states passed laws governing assignment for the benefit of creditors, which is very similar to bankruptcy except that it is administered under the supervision of a state court instead of a federal bankruptcy court. Technically, an assignment for the benefit of creditors is the transfer by an insolvent debtor of all his property to an assignee, who agrees to hold that property and its profits in trust for the benefit of the debtor's creditors, and if there is anything left over, to pay the balance back to the debtor. (In every large American city I would say there are about 10,000 bankruptcies for every one assignment for the benefit of creditors.)

assumption of risk. A defense made by a defendant in a NEGLIGENCE action, consisting of a claim that the plaintiff was injured by a condition or set of facts of which he was aware, and that he thus voluntarily assumed the risk of injury and therefore may not recover DAMAGES.

assured. The person to whom an insurance policy is issued.

attachment. A remedy given a creditor during a suit against a debtor whereby the creditor is permitted by law to seize the debtor's property and turn it over to a court officer so that if a judgment is rendered in favor of the creditor, the property will be available to satisfy that judgment. An attachment is often confused with an EXECUTION, but they are essentially different. An execution is used to enforce a judgment *after* it is obtained; an attachment is used *before* the judgment to hold property pending the outcome of the suit.

Generally, an attachment may be had only in actions for money damages. There has to be some special reason for an attachment, such as the fact that the debtor has left the state or is about to leave the state, or that he has concealed himself or property with intent to defraud creditors. Sometimes a fraudulent transfer of property is the ground for attachment. False representation by a debtor as to his financial condition may also be a ground for attachment.

Most property (including merchandise, fixtures in a store, money, crops, rolling stock of railroads, bonds, liquor, books, manufactured goods, judgments, and real estate in general) is subject to attachment.

Example: Mr. Apple sues Mr. Plum for $20,000 due on a promissory note. Plum owns a lot of real estate. He deeds one house to his wife for "love and affection." He sells another house to a cousin for a paltry sum and is having a lawyer draw up a deed of another house to his brother-in-law. Plum is a merchant who operates a very profitable business. Apple has his lawyer draw up an affidavit telling about Plum's transfer of property with intent to defraud Plum's creditors. A court attachment is issued, putting a LIEN on the merchandise and fixtures in Plum's store, which prevents Plum from making any transfer of the merchandise and fixtures until the lawsuit is settled.

attainder, bill of. See BILL.

attorney-at-law. There are two classifications of attorneys: ATTORNEYS IN FACT and attorneys-at-law.

An attorney-at-law is a lawyer. He is an officer of a court of justice who advises clients or conducts court proceedings.

Despite Watergate and other public scandals involving lawyers, the rank and file of private attorneys-at-law maintains a high standard of ethics in respect to both their clients and their duties as officers of the court. Attorneys-at-law have an obligation to the court to see that their cases before it are disposed on the merits, free from corruption and fraud or technical errors. For over a hundred years, ending in 1970, lawyers lived under a Canon of Ethics, which, being outdated, was then supplanted by a new code known as the Code of Professional Responsibility. This code has over fifty rules of conduct required of attorneys. Generally, under the code an attorney-at-law is bound to maintain the integrity and competence of the legal profession. He is bound to respect the confidences and secrets of his client (see CONFIDENTIAL RELATION), to REPRESENT his client competently and within the law, and to preserve the identity of funds and property of his client. Above all, he is required to seek to improve the legal and judicial system. If you want to know more about the Code of Professional Responsibility, you may write the American Bar Association (1155 East 60th Street, Chicago, Illinois 60639) and ask them to send you a copy of the code.

Amendments to the new code must be made from time to time because of rulings of the United States Supreme Court. For example, the code had to be modified when the Court ruled that the code's restriction on lawyers' advertising was unconstitutional as an abridgment of free speech. In other words, lawyers can now advertise.

For certain misconduct, criminal or otherwise, an attorney-at-law may be suspended from the practice of law for a certain length of time or may be disbarred. DISBARMENT is almost the worst thing that can happen to an attorney professionally, and is likely to be the end of his legal career.

attorney general. The chief law officer of the United States. Each state also has an attorney general, who is the chief law officer for that state.

attorney in fact. An agent who acts for a special purpose or for general purposes under a written authorization called a *power of attorney.*

attractive nuisance. A doctrine in tort law that imposes an obligation on a person to guard against instrumentalities and conditions that attract children and may endanger them.

Example: The Excelsior Railroad Company maintains an unfenced and unguarded railroad trestle adjacent to a neighborhood with many young children. Johnny Smith, an eight-year-old boy, and his companions frequently use the trestle as a means to cross over a highway. Johnny used the trestle in a game of follow-the-leader. He slipped and fell 50 feet to the highway below, sustaining serious injuries. The railroad was liable for damages sustained by Johnny and should have taken means to protect immature children from injury for use of the trestle, which under certain circumstances was a "dangerous instrumentality."

aviation law. As we all know, aviation is the art or science of flying. Flying starts from a local airport, but in nine cases out of ten it soon develops into an interstate operation. Although the owner of land for most purposes owns the airspace above the land, for aviation purposes all air is navigable unless some special harm is caused or threatened to the owner of land below.

The federal government, rather than individual states, has the paramount right to regulate air traffic. Congress, which by virtue of the COMMERCE clause of the United States Constitution, has the power to control and regulate aviation, enacted legislation delegating that power to the Civil Aeronautics Board and Federal Aviation Authority.

Safety is a very important factor in flying. All air accidents are investigated by the Federal Aviation Authority and the National Transportation Safety Board. Federal laws require that all aircraft be registered and numbered. Federally licensed inspectors examine aircraft and certify them for airworthiness. The federal government licenses qualified pilots and controls private and public airports, hangars, and other aviation facilities.

Air traffic control is under the jurisdiction of the federal government. Air traffic controllers are federal employees, and the United States may thus be liable for the NEGLIGENCE of an air traffic controller that causes injury to a plane or its occupants. Such negligence may consist of failure to provide a pilot with sufficient weather information, failure to use radar or other safety equipment, failure to comply with government regulations, failure to give adequate information and instructions to a pilot, failure to give proper warning of danger to a pilot, failure to advise of the presence of other aircraft, etc.

B

bail. May be either a person or an amount of money or property given to secure the release of a prisoner from jail or to pledge a prisoner's appearance in court at a certain time and place.

The granting of bail keeps an accused person from having to go to jail or permits him to be released from jail and theoretically transfers that person to his bail (a person).

In the ordinary case, bail is fixed by the court. It sometimes is refused in the case of a CAPITAL CRIME or if the evidence of guilt is overwhelming. Courts also in their discretion may deny bail where there appears to be some risk or threat to public safety if the accused is given liberty.

It is usually within the court's discretion whether or not to free a convicted criminal on bail pending an appeal or a motion for a new trial. There are many factors that may affect the court's granting bail pending an appeal, including the possibility of the reversal of the conviction by an appellate court, the nature of the crime, the character and record of the person convicted, etc.

The United States Constitution (Eighth Amendment) provides that "excessive bail shall not be required," but excessive is not defined. Under certain circumstances bail ranging from $500 to $1,000 has been held to be excessive, whereas under other circumstances bail ranging from $2,000 to $250,000 has been held not excessive.

See also RECOGNIZANCE.

bail bond. An obligation by the accused and his sureties, which may become null and void after the accused person performs the acts required by the court. The purpose of a bail bond is to compel the presence of the accused at the required time.

bailiff. An official to whom some authority or jurisdiction is granted; generally in the United States a court officer.

bailment. A CONTRACT for the delivery and redelivery of goods for some purpose. The person who delivers the goods is the bailor, and the person to whom the goods are delivered is the bailee. An example of a bailment is John Jones delivering a suit of clothes to the ABC Drycleaning Company for the purpose of cleaning and pressing.

In a bailment there is no transfer of ownership, simply a transfer of custody from the bailor to the bailee. A bailment may be verbal, and no particular form of contract is required.

Although a bailee is not an insurer of the property, he is liable for NEGLIGENCE in his handling of the property. If the bailee is without fault, however, he is not liable for the loss or destruction of the property.

Example: When Dick Smith parked his car in the Excelsior parking lot, which allowed its employees to sit in parked cars and smoke, one of the employees recklessly allowed cigarette sparks to ignite the auto upholstery, substantially damaging Smith's car. The Excelsior Parking Company was liable for the damage to the auto.

banc. The full court or the full BENCH of a court. When a court sits *en banc,* all the judges of the court convene; this is distinguished, for example, from the sitting of one or two judges of a court made up of ten judges.

banking laws. Banking laws are stringent, and little wonder. In the early days of the United States there was financial and moral chaos and turmoil, largely due to the loose and irresponsible handling of banks. In retrospect, it is almost unbelievable how unscrupulous and greedy our so-called bankers were. Banks issued currency, much of which became worthless, then induced people to borrow money, and then "called" debts and foreclosed mortgages. All across the country the craze for irresponsible banking spread like wildfire. In 1816 there were over 246 state banks, which issued paper money. Speculation was rampant. People were encouraged to sell their property for worthless bank currency, and bankruptcies were prevalent.

Eventually, state legislators issued regulations to control banks so that they became what they were intended to be: vital commercial links in the capitalistic system. Eventually they became essentially institutions for the deposit of money and the granting of loans.

In 1913 Congress created the Federal Reserve System. In 1933, after the Depression banking debacle, a corporation was created, the Federal

Deposit Insurance Corporation, which insured the deposits of certain banks.

Time was when the owners of banks generally were in such poor public favor that most states had laws that imposed double liability upon stockholders of banks to depositors and creditors; that is, there was a liability in addition to the liability a stockholder of an ordinary corporation had in paying at least the SUBSCRIPTION to the stock of the corporation.

Banks have broad powers, including the right to solicit deposits, to act as administrators or executors of estates, to act as trustees, to enter into contracts, to act as agents or brokers in connection with the ordinary business of the bank, to lend money, to buy and sell real estate for places of bank business and for the protection of loans, to purchase commercial paper, to borrow money (with restrictions), to transfer money or credit for their customers by means of cable, wireless, telegraph, or otherwise. Generally a bank can issue a *letter of credit* (a letter requesting some person or institution to advance money or credit to a customer of the bank, which the bank promises to repay to whoever advances the money). Bank laws have done away with and prohibit the issuance of bank notes, formerly circulated as currency.

Banks sometimes act as agents for their customers in collecting and obtaining payment of commercial paper. Banks have the general authority to undertake the collection of commercial paper as an incident of bank business.

Fundamentally, most banks are in the business of receiving deposits of money from customers; that is the starting point of most banking business. It creates the relationship of the bank as a debtor and the customer as a creditor.

In general, banks are owned by stockholders, but mutual savings banks are owned by the bank depositors. Such banks are operated by trustees, directors, and managers.

bankrupt. An insolvent person who is unable to pay his debts as they mature.

bankruptcy laws. The United States Constitution gives Congress the right to pass laws on the subject of bankruptcy. Until recently the prevailing legislation was the Bankruptcy Act of 1898 as amended in 1938 by the Chandler Act. This was superseded by the Bankruptcy Reform Act of 1978 (effective October 1, 1979), which simplified bankruptcy law and practice.

bar. The whole body of members of the legal profession. The term was probably derived from the railing, or "bar," in English courtrooms which separated lawyers, judges, jurors, and others connected with the trial of a court case from the general public.

bar association. An organization composed of members of the legal profession. The association which speaks for all lawyers in the United States is called the American Bar Association. Each state has its own bar association, and most counties (there are scores of them in some states) also have bar associations.

In many states there are so-called integrated or compulsory bars, which means lawyers must join the bar associations in order to practice law. Other states have voluntary bar associations, membership in which is not required in order to practice law.

barratry. 1. According to English common law, the stirring up of quarrels or litigation. **2.** In ADMIRALTY LAW, a violation of duty by the captain or crew against the interests of the ship owners.

barrister. According to English law, a trial lawyer. In England the court lawyer is the barrister, while a SOLICITOR is the office lawyer. In the United States there is no such distinction. Here all lawyers are licensed to appear in court.

bastard. An illegitimate child. The law creates a presumption in favor of the legitimacy of a child born in wedlock—this means the child is presumed the husband's child.

Change in the status of a bastard to that of a lawfully born child is called legitimation. How legitimation is effected varies from state to state. Generally, a bastard is entitled to inherit property from the mother. The United States Supreme Court has held that the laws of some states are unconstitutional in denying rights of inheritance to bastards. The same court has held constitutional the laws of other states that permit legitimation, which protects bastards. States have bastardy proceedings to compel the illegitimate child's father to acknowledge paternity and contribute to the child's support.

battery. See ASSAULT AND BATTERY.

bench. The seat of judges or the COURT itself. The terms "bench" and BAR refer to judges and lawyers: Bench means judges collectively and bar means lawyers as a whole.

bench warrant. An order from the court directing the proper legal officer to arrest a person.

beneficial association. An organization formed primarily for the relief of its members in time of sickness or need and for the care of families of deceased members. The organization may or may not be incorporated. It may not be organized for profit.

Members of beneficial associations generally are assessed dues. Funds collected may be invested, and the benefits are payable to needy members or the families of deceased members.

Example: A group of citizens living in the state of New Jersey organized a beneficial association and called it Fraternal Brothers. Each member is assessed $10 a month. The bylaws of the association provide that in the event of an illness that prevents a member from working, that member receives $100 a month sickness benefit. When a member dies, his widow or other designated beneficiary is paid $100 a month for life. There are 30,000 members of the organization, and the plan works.

beneficiary. One for whose benefit a trust is created; also the person to whom a policy of insurance is payable.

bequeath. To give personal property by will. See also DEVISE.

bequest. A gift made by a WILL. In some jurisdictions this term refers to a gift of personal property by will, while DEVISE refers to a gift of real estate by will.

best evidence rule. In the law of evidence, a rule that the most persuasive EVIDENCE (generally the original document) should be used rather than some other SECONDARY EVIDENCE.

> *Example:* A sues B for BREACH OF CONTRACT. Normally the contract itself should be produced. If the contract is not available, a copy may be used, but that is secondary evidence, not the best evidence.

beyond a reasonable doubt. A phrase used in criminal law, it means satisfied to a moral certainty. The rule is that the prosecution must prove beyond a reasonable doubt—but not necessarily to a mathematical certainty—that the accused committed a crime. If the jury or other finder of facts has any doubt as to the guilt of the accused, then the VERDICT must be in favor of the accused.

bigamy. The crime of having two living spouses. The essence of the crime is that the person entering into a second marriage knows that the first marriage is still valid. There may be a good defense to a charge of bigamy if the person charged honestly believed that his former spouse was dead or divorced.

bill. A formal written statement. It may be a pleading in a lawsuit, a proposed action of the legislature, an invoice, or a variety of other things in different contexts. The following are examples of various types of bills:

> *In litigation:* Originally a term used to mean the original pleading, such as a declaration or complaint.
>
> A *bill of costs* is an itemized statement of statutory expenses charged against the unsuccessful party.
>
> A *bill of particulars* is a written statement of the facts claimed by a party, showing dates, amounts, and other facts in detail, which is given to amplify the pleading.
>
> *In legislation:* Proposed law.
>
> A *bill of attainder* is a legislative act by which a person is pronounced guilty of a crime without trial or conviction. It is prohibited by the United States Constitution.
>
> *In commercial law:* A *bill payable* is an obligation owed by a person

or business. A *bill receivable* is an account owing to a person or business.

A *bill of lading* is an instrument signed by a common carrier stating the terms for the delivery of merchandise. It actually is a receipt for goods, specifying the contract for their delivery.

A *bill of sale* is a written instrument by which one person transfers to another rights in personal property.

In criminal law: A *bill of indictment* is a formal, written document whereby the grand jury accuses a person of committing a crime.

In constitutional law: The *Bill of Rights* is the first ten amendments to the federal Constitution; it guarantees individual rights and privileges. State constitutions also have bills of rights. See CONSTITUTIONAL LAW.

bill of particulars. See under BILL—IN LITIGATION.

Bill of Rights. See CONSTITUTIONAL LAW.

bills and notes. A branch of law relating to NEGOTIABLE instruments. A negotiable instrument is a legal document, title to which may be transferred merely by delivery or indorsement instead of a formal ASSIGNMENT. The law of negotiable instruments is a good example of how American law changes over the years. Originally the handling of negotiable paper by merchants was governed by a body of law called the Law Merchant. Then in the latter part of the nineteenth century the Commission on Uniform State Laws prepared what was known as the Negotiable Instruments Law (N.I.L.), which was in effect for a good part of a century and was eventually adopted by all the states. The wheels of change turned slowly, and the N.I.L. was supplanted in the 1960s by the Uniform Commercial Code (U.C.C.), which in principle has been adopted by all of the states except Louisiana. The U.C.C. covers not only the law of negotiable instruments but the law of other commercial activities, such as sales, secured transactions, warehouses, banking, etc. *Commercial paper* includes most negotiable instruments, such as bank checks, promissory notes, and other bills of exchange that today are controlled by the U.C.C.

Certain kinds of commercial paper may be non-negotiable and yet legally valid.

Example: A promissory note may be negotiable if payable to the order of John Jones. All that Jones has to do to transfer the ownership of the promissory note to some other person is to INDORSE the back side of the note. On the other hand, the promissory note may be conditional. Suppose the maker of the promissory note makes it payable to Jones if Jones rents his summer cottage to Paul Smith for the month of August. That makes the promissory note non-negotiable but still valid. If Jones rents the summer cottage to Smith for the month of August, the maker of the promissory note has made a valid contract to pay Jones the face amount of the promissory note.

The most common form of a bill of exchange is a bank check. In the case of a bill of exchange there are ordinarily three parties: (a) the drawer, (b) the payee, and (c) the drawee. In the case of a bank check, the drawer is the one who has the bank account, the drawee is the bank, and the payee is the person to whom the check is payable.

There are a number of intricate requirements to determine whether commercial paper such as a bank check, promissory note, etc., is negotiable.

It is possible today to provide in a promissory note or other negotiable instrument that if the instrument is not paid at maturity, the holder of the note may collect an attorney's fee or the cost of collection in addition to the face amount of the instrument. Such a provision does not affect the negotiability or validity of the instrument.

The maker may put up collateral as security for a negotiable instrument or give a mortgage on real estate to secure the note.

binder. A brief outline of an agreement pending the issuance of a formal agreement. For example, in the insurance business a binder may be issued by an agent to give temporary protection to the insured pending the issuance of a policy.

A binder is also used in real estate transactions when a person who makes a down payment on the purchase of a home is given a receipt that outlines the essential terms of the purchase agreement.

Blackacre (Whiteacre). Fictitious names used to designate parcels of land. Compare DOE, JOHN (JANE).

blackmail. The EXTORTION or the exaction of money under threat of bodily injury or of disclosure of alleged wrongdoing.

blood. Family relationship by birth. *Half blood* is a degree of relationship between those who have the same mother *or* the same father, but not the same mother *and* father. *Whole blood* relationship is the degree of relationship among people having all the same antecedents.

blue laws. Legislation that severely restricts commercial activities on Sunday. Blue laws originated in the colony of Connecticut in prerevolutionary days.

blue-sky laws. State laws regulating investments, for the protection of investors from sellers of questionable oil wells and mining stock and other fraudulent schemes.

> *Example:* New York state under the leadership of Attorney General Louis Lefkowitz enforced laws prohibiting fraudulent schemes hazardous to investors.

board. A group of persons organized under law to perform official duties—

e.g., board of education, board of health, board of directors. Generally the governing body of a CORPORATION is a board of directors. The officers of a corporation are responsible to the board of directors. The stockholders are the owners of the corporation and elect the board of directors.

bodily injury. INJURY to the human body (e.g., a bruise, a cut, a wound). In insurance parlance, a claim for bodily injury is referred to as a "b.i." claim, as distinguished from a "p.d." claim, which is a claim for property damage. See TRAUMA.

bona. A Latin word meaning goods or property. When a sheriff or constable is told by an EXECUTION to levy on the property of a judgment debtor, and he finds no property on which he can levy and sell, he notes on the execution "Nulla bona" (or "N.B.").

bona fide. Good faith. Although the phrase has been popularized and is generally understood in nonlegal matters, as a legal phrase it is applied particularly to FRAUD cases. Simply stated, *bona fide* means good faith as distinguished from bad faith. In law *bona fide* applies to motive and intention. For example, a *bona fide* purchaser is an innocent buyer of property who purchases without notice or knowledge of facts that would invalidate the title to the property.

bond. A CONTRACT to pay money. It may be issued by individuals, corporations, municipalities, or businesses. The person who gives the bond is known as the obligor. The person to whom payment is to be made is known as the obligee.

The only necessary parties to a bond are the obligor and the obligee, but sometimes bonds have sureties who guarantee the payment of the bond.

Bonds may have a *condition,* such as that on the performance of a certain act the bonds shall be void. For example, in the case of a BAIL BOND for the release of a prisoner held in jail, the condition of the bond would be that if the prisoner appears in court on the trial of the case or otherwise performs the directions of the court, the bond is void. Otherwise the bond would be in full force and effect, and the obligor on the bond would be liable.

Bonds are sometimes NEGOTIABLE; that is, they may be transferred or sold by mere delivery. Such bonds may be payable to bearer, and may have attached coupons which are payable on specified interest dates. Those coupons may be clipped and deposited in banks in the same way as money. Hence the saying, with reference to a wealthy person: "He spends his time clipping coupons."

Generally a bond has a SEAL, which makes it rather fancy though not necessarily more legal.

book of original entries. The first permanent record of a business transaction. It is a requirement of the law of EVIDENCE that in order for a book of account to be admitted in evidence it must be the book of original entry.

book value. The value of the assets as shown on the books of a CORPORATION or business company (original value less depreciation) less the LIABILITIES of the corporation or company shown on its books. The book value of stock may be far different from the actual market value.

> *Example:* The ABC Real Estate Corporation's principal assets are 10 pieces of real estate purchased 10 years ago. Each year the corporation had depreciated the value of the real estate 3% of the purchase price of the real estate. Therefore, the book value of the STOCK of the corporation is 70% of the amount paid for the real estate less the liabilities of the corporation. Since the corporation bought the 10 parcels of real estate, they have tripled in value. Therefore the actual value of the stock of the corporation is over 4 times its book value.

bottomry. A contract in ADMIRALTY LAW whereby a ship and its contents are pledged as security for a loan, but the loan is repaid only if the ship survives a particular trip.

boundary. A line separating two parcels of REAL ESTATE; often it is a line running between what are called MONUMENTS.

bounty. A sum of money or other reward promised by a government, generally the state or federal legislature, in order to encourage some action. In American history probably the most general form of bounty was that for military service; such bounties were prevalent during the Civil War. Bounties have also been awarded for the destruction of vicious or noxious animals, for the settlement of land, and for planting trees and shrubbery. When the government offers a bounty for the performance of some service, the person performing that service is entitled to the bounty and may have a CAUSE OF ACTION against the government if the bounty is not paid.

boycott. In labor relations law there are two kinds of boycotts, primary boycott and secondary boycott.

A *primary boycott* exists when a union by concerted action stops or attempts to stop people from doing business with the union members' employer. A primary boycott is legal under the National Labor Relations Act. A *secondary boycott* is pressure brought by union members on customers of the union members' employer to withhold all patronage from middlemen who deal in the employer's product. A secondary boycott is illegal as an *unfair labor practice* under the Taft-Hartley Act.

breach of contract. Failure to fulfill contractual obligation. If the part of the CONTRACT that is not fulfilled is very formal, it is called a *breach of* COVENANT.

If a party to a contract makes a positive statement or expresses an intention that he will not perform the contract, that is called an *anticipatory breach of contract*.

breach of the peace. A disturbance of the public tranquility, generally involving acts of violence that cause public alarm. Often, breach of the peace is used as a catchall charge; for example, when there is some technical defense to another criminal activity.

breach of promise. A popular expression for breaking a promise to marry. In the early twentieth century lawsuits were frequently brought for breach of promise, but they have since been abolished as legal remedies by many states.

breach of trust. Any act done by a FIDUCIARY in violation of the terms of his TRUST or contrary to the basic rules for the performance of his fiduciary duties.

breach of warranty. A breach that generally applies to deeds of real estate for which a WARRANTY deed is given. A warranty deed essentially is the guarantee that the seller has good TITLE to the land which he conveys. If there is a defect in the title to the land, there is a breach of warranty. This does not involve FRAUD on the part of the seller. It simply means that the seller is unable to fulfill his contract to deliver good title.

breaking and entering. See BURGLARY.

bribery. 1. The giving or **2.** the receipt of something of value to influence a person in his public or corporate duties. Under most state laws even the promise to give or receive something of value may constitute a crime. The average bribe involves money, but there can be many substitutes for money in the crime.

brief. A written argument of facts and laws to convince a court of the justice and merit of a litigant's position. To *brief an issue* is to write such an argument, complete with as much CITATION of prior cases as possible.

broker. A person who works for others on a commercial basis to negotiate the sale or disposition of property. He himself does not have possession or control of property. There are many kinds of brokers: insurance, real estate, stock, etc.

Generally the seller pays the broker his commission, although in some arrangements it is the buyer who pays. The amount of the broker's commission is fixed by contract, but sometimes custom regulates it. A state government can regulate or license the business of any kind of broker.

building and loan association. A company (CORPORATION or PARTNERSHIP) that loans money to its members to assist them in building homes. The money is raised from among its members by means of STOCK SUBSCRIPTIONS. Building and loan associations became popular in the United States in the nineteenth century and now exist in most American states.

There are various types of building and loan associations. Federal law governs one type, and there are building and loan association laws in the various states.

bulk sales laws. Statutes passed by the legislatures of the various states that regulate merchants who sell a stock or goods in bulk.

burden of proof. The obligation of a party in a lawsuit to prove a certain fact at issue in the case. Normally a plaintiff has the burden of proving his case, and if the plaintiff fails to sustain that burden, the defendant wins the case. In the law of EVIDENCE, burden of proof may sometimes shift from the plaintiff to the defendant or back and forth between the parties to the lawsuit. It is a complicated doctrine.

burglary. Burglary is defined differently by the laws of various states, but in general it is *breaking and entering* a building for the purpose of committing a crime. In order for there to be a breaking, an alleged burglar must use some force. Thus if the owner or occupant of a building leaves the entrance door open or unlocked and the alleged burglar simply walks in, there may be *illegal entry* but no breaking. The crime of burglary is punishable by the laws of the various states according to the *degree* involved. Degrees of burglary may depend on whether the burglar was armed, whether the building was entered in the nighttime, whether the building was a dwelling house, etc.

business trust (Massachusetts trust). A plan whereby under the terms of a declaration of trust, property is transferred to trustees, who manage the property for the benefit of others.

bylaws. Regulations or rules adopted by an association or a corporation for the intended convenience of such corporation or association. When lawyers prepare bylaws for an organization, they often include statements of the laws governing the organization so that when its officers want to take some action, they can consult the bylaws to determine the legal procedures.

> *Example:* The laws of a particular state require that stockholders of a corporation be given 10 days' notice of a special stockholders' meeting to decide whether a particular piece of real estate should be sold. The bylaws provide that the stockholders shall receive 10 days' advance notice of a special stockholders' meeting. Since the bylaws conform to the state law, the president and secretary simply follow the requirement of the bylaws and send each stockholder of the corporation a written notice that a stockholders' meeting will be held 10 days hence to decide upon the sale of a particular parcel of the corporation's real estate.

C

---

calendar, court. An arrangement of cases to be tried before a court listed according to the DATE OF ISSUE.

canon. A canon is a law or rule of a church. Canon law is a body of ecclesiastical jurisprudence.

capacity. The qualification or competency of persons or corporations to perform certain acts, depending on their age or mental condition. In the case of corporations, capacity may depend on the provisions of the corporate CHARTER. Compare ULTRA VIRES.

capita. See PER CAPITA.

capital crime. A crime for which the maximum penalty is death.

Although the United States Supreme Court in 1972 held that the death penalty was unconstitutional in certain situations, it held in 1976 that the death penalty is not unconstitutional *per se*—only where it is MANDATORY for certain crimes and the guidelines for imposing it are not followed. A jury or other sentencing authority may consider the circumstances and recommend whether or not a death sentence should be imposed.

capital gain. Income that results from the sale of principal assets. If a capital asset is held for more than one year and then sold, the gain is called long-term capital gain, and under United States income tax laws is taxed at more favorable rates than ordinary income.

capital stock. The amount of STOCK issued, or authorized to be issued, by a CORPORATION charter.

capitalization of income. A method of valuing property such as real estate.

Using a factor selected by experts who take into consideration the type of property and location involved, property is capitalized by multiplying the income of the property by that factor.

Example: If the net income of a parcel of real estate is $10,000 and the arbitrary factor is 10, the capitalized value of the property is $100,000.

care. A general dictionary has a number of meanings for the word "care." In law, however, the word is used to mean attention, diligence, or discretion. In differing situations the law requires various degrees of care. *Ordinary care* means the care which an ordinary, reasonable, careful, and prudent person would use under similar circumstances. See REASONABLE MAN.

carnal knowledge. Sexual intercourse. ("Knowledge" is an archaic expression for sexual intercourse.) In law the phrase is used in RAPE and ADULTERY cases.

carrier. **1.** A company that issues INSURANCE policies. **2.** A person or a corporation transporting property or persons for hire. A *common carrier* is a facility presented to the public as transporting persons or property for hire. Common carriers include buses, vans, trucks, railroads, streetcars, taxicabs, steamboats, airplanes, etc. The law imposes a number of obligations and duties on a common carrier. If it does not fulfill these, the carrier may be liable for DAMAGES.

In the early development of the United States, common carriers such as railroads, express companies, and buses were prime targets of people seeking damages. The law imposed a duty on common carriers to use extreme care in transporting persons or property for hire.

A common carrier can be engaged in transporting people and every sort of property, including money and other valuables, luggage, merchandise, manufactured goods, livestock, etc. Regulations galore sprang up in the nineteenth century, and today all kinds of carriers are regulated in great detail by the federal INTERSTATE COMMERCE COMMISSION, in addition to regulations of the public service commissions of various states.

A common carrier is bound to exercise CARE and is liable for NEGLIGENCE injuring persons or property.

A common carrier has the obligation to load and unload freight. It ordinarily is liable for injury to or loss of property which it undertakes to transport except in the case of an ACT OF GOD or acts of public enemies or government authority. The courts have refused to approve attempts of common carriers by notices or fine print to limit their legal LIABILITY.

case. A lawsuit before a court of justice to determine the rights of the litigants.

case law. Law established by decisions made by judges, as distinguished from statutes passed by the legislature. See JUDGE-MADE LAW and COMMON LAW.

case method. A method of teaching law by the study of actual court cases, as distinguished from the method of teaching law by textbooks. The case method was started at Harvard Law School in 1869 and is now used in most American lawschools.

casualty. An accident resulting in death, personal injury, or damage to property, or destruction from a shipwreck, fire, storm, or lightning.

causa mortis. A Latin phrase ("in case of death") which generally applies to gifts. A GIFT *causa mortis* is effective only if the person making the gift dies. If the person making the gift survives, the gift is ineffective.

> *Example:* John Smith, on what he supposed was his deathbed, gave his diamond ring to his friend Howard Brown, saying, "Howard, I want you to have this ring if I die." Smith recovered from what he had thought was a fatal illness. The gift was a gift *causa mortis,* and because Smith survived the illness, Brown must give the ring back to Smith.

cause célèbre. A French phrase meaning "celebrated case." A cause célèbre is a court case or decision which is unusual because of the prominence of the parties involved, sensational evidence, or other notoriety.

cause of action. 1. A right to sue. **2.** A statement of facts sufficient to justify a court in rendering a judgment.

caveat. A Latin word meaning "let him beware," used with other Latin words: e.g., *caveat emptor,* "let the buyer beware," and *caveat venditor,* "let the seller beware." Often used by itself in phrases like "with the following *caveat,*" meaning word of caution.

In some states a formal objection to probating a will is called a *caveat.*

cease and desist. A phrase used by regulatory agencies ordering a person to stop some action. If the person does not stop the action complained of, the regulatory agency may apply to a court to compel him to cease and desist the action. Then if the person does not stop the action, he may be punished for CONTEMPT OF COURT.

center of gravity. See CONFLICT OF LAWS.

cert. denied. See CERTIORARI.

certiorari. **1.** A writ issued by a high court calling on a lower (or inferior) court to deliver the record of a case for review. *Certiorari* is a form of appeal. The best-known example is the kind in which an aggrieved party petitions the United States Supreme Court to review his or her case. Many people who go to court say, "I will fight this case to the Supreme Court," but going to the United States Supreme Court is not easy. The law books are full of cases which end "Cert. denied," meaning that *certiorari* was denied by the Supreme Court—it refused to call for the lower court's records, with which it would have reviewed the case.

2. A court review of the action of a branch of government or of an administrative agency.

> *Example:* The City of Jonestown assesses a vacant lot owned by John Smith at $10,000. Smith claims the assessment is excessive and brings *certiorari* proceeding in superior court, claiming that the property is worth only $5,000. The superior court hears testimony as to the true value of the property and makes a decision, fixing the value at $7,500.

cestui qui trust. See TRUST.

chain of title. A list of documents that make up purported ownership of real estate, each document constituting a link in the chain of title. See ABSTRACTS OF TITLE.

chambers. The private office of a judge.

champerty. The buying of an interest in litigation by someone who is not a party to it.

chancery. Obsolete term used to designate a branch of the court handling EQUITY cases. The word originally referred to the king's chancellor, to whom the king referred such cases.

change of venue. The removal of a court case by court order from one locality (e.g., a county or district) to another. The grounds for a change of venue may be (a) the convenience of witnesses or (b) the claim that a fair and impartial trial cannot be obtained in the original county or district.

charge to a jury. See INSTRUCTION.

charitable contributions. In tax law, charitable contributions to churches, hospitals, educational institutions, branches of government, etc., as defined by the Internal Revenue Code, are deductible from one's gross income for income tax purposes.

charitable organization. An organization that meets the test of the Internal Revenue Code (I.R.C.) as exempt from taxation; generally a benevolent or philanthropic nonprofit organization that meets other requirements—for example, tax-exempt organizations may not engage in lobbying. See NONPROFIT.

charter. In modern law, a certificate of incorporation, or a grant of power by the government to a municipality or government agency. A charter specifies the powers and responsibilities of a corporate or government agency.

charter party. A contract by which the owner of a ship or vessel leases the ship or vessel to another party. See ADMIRALTY LAW.

chattel. An article of personal property.

chattel annexed to realty. See FIXTURE.

chattel mortgage. A transfer of an interest in personal property as security for a debt. The essential elements of a chattel mortgage document are (a) the parties to the loan, (b) the description of the property transferred as security for the debt, and (c) the amount of the loan and how it is to be paid. If the mortgage debt is not paid, the holder of the mortgage has a right to sell the property to satisfy the debt.

check-off system. In United States LABOR RELATIONS LAW, the deduction of union dues and other payments, such as credit union monies, from the wages of an employee by an employer, who then pays them to the labor union, credit union, or other person designated by the employee.

chose **in action** An intangible claim. It is to be distinguished from tangible property.

> *Example:* Jim Jones sold Sam Smith a horse for $500. In exchange for the horse, Jones took Smith's note for $500. Smith now owns the horse. That is tangible personal property. Jones now holds Smith's note for $500. That is a *chose* in action.

circumstantial evidence. EVIDENCE of facts and circumstances from which the existence or nonexistence of a fact may be inferred.

> *Example:* If one of the points in a lawsuit was whether or not John Jones was at a certain house at a certain time, the facts that his car was seen in front of the house at the time in question and his gloves were found in the house might be considered circumstantial evidence from which an inference could be drawn that he was at that house at the time in question, even though there is no direct proof, such as an eyewitness, of his having been there.

citation. 1. A notice issued by a court requiring a person to appear in court on a certain day or to show cause why he should not do as the court directs.

> *Example:* When a will is offered for probate, the court issues a citation directing all persons who might be affected by the will to show cause on a specified date if they contend that the will should not be admitted to probate.

2. The QUOTATION of a legal authority in support of a proposition of law.

citizen's arrest. Arrest by a private person (without a warrant) because of the commission of a felony or breach of the peace where the person making the arrest knows or has reasonable grounds to believe that such a felony or breach of the peace has taken place.

> *Example:* Jones observes Smith breaking a jewelry store window and

stealing valuable pieces of jewelry. Jones is at liberty to arrest Smith for the act of stealing the jewelry.

civil action. An adversary proceeding for the enforcement of a right or the redressing of a wrong. The action calls for a trial of the issues framed by a COMPLAINT and the denial or admission set forth in the acts. A civil action is generally a private legal proceeding, as opposed to a criminal action.

civil law. 1. The Roman law or system of law later adopted by France, Italy, Spain, Quebec, South American countries, and the state of Louisiana. Compare COMMON LAW. **2.** Law applied to civil cases as distinguished from criminal law.

civil rights. 1. Rights of individual citizens. There are a number of civil rights guaranteed by the United States Constitution, including the right to due process of law, the right to personal liberty, the right to worship, freedom to vote, freedom of speech, freedom of the press.

2. The term has come to apply particularly to the rights of minority groups. Although the Thirteenth, Fourteenth, and Fifteenth Amendments to the United States Constitution in the 1860s and 1870s abolished slavery and gave equal rights to all citizens, as a practical matter black people were denied the right to vote, and they were denied many other privileges of white people until the middle of the twentieth century. Jim Crow railroad cars persisted, and some states had dual systems of education, one system for black and another for white children. As late as 1896 in the famous case of *Plessy* v. *Ferguson,* the United States Supreme Court upheld segregation in a railroad transport case. In that case Justice Harlan dissented from the majority ruling of the Court, which held that separate but equal facilities were constitutional; Harlan said, "Our Constitution is color-blind." Although some state courts and a few lower federal courts protested, it was not until 1954 that the U.S. Supreme Court, in the then startling case of *Brown* v. *Board of Education of Topeka,* held that "separate but equal" systems of education were unconstitutional and ordered DESEGREGATION of public schools.

Civil rights affect all areas of living—transportation, the use of public facilities, employment, housing, etc.

Today civil rights are protected by numerous federal laws that prohibit all kinds of discrimination. Public accommodations and facilities are available to people of whatever race, color, nationality, sex, or religion. There are many federally assisted programs to help the poor and disadvantaged obtain equal employment rights and fair housing.

civil service. The administrative body of government that performs other than military functions.

claimant. One who claims a right or a sum of money.

class action. A legal ACTION brought on behalf of the plaintiff and other persons similarly situated; a lawsuit in which one or more persons sue on behalf of themselves and other persons affected by the alleged injury. Some courts have specific requirements for class actions, and if those requirements are met, the class action is certified by the court as carried on for the benefit of certain people. For example, a woman editor at XYZ Publishing Company may sue her employer on behalf of herself and the other women editors for equal pay with the male editors. It is a class action because the other women have not joined her in making the claim, but they will benefit from it.

clean hands. An expression used in a court of EQUITY, meaning that the person who seeks equitable relief must be free from FRAUD, unjust conduct, or other wrongful doing.

clear title. Valid and indisputable TITLE to REAL ESTATE, free from all doubts, liens, and encumbrances. See ABSTRACTS OF TITLE and CHAIN OF TITLE.

clemency. See PARDON.

clerk. 1. A term formerly used to designate a law student in the office of a practicing attorney. Such a student is no longer referred to as a clerk but is now known as an associate. 2. A person who assists a judge in court.

clerk of the court. An officer of a court in charge of keeping records, entering judgments, etc.

close (closed) corporation. A CORPORATION whose stock is not publicly owned and is generally held by only a few individuals.

closed shop. An arrangement arrived at between management and a union whereby an employee must be a member of the union as a precondition to work for the company. Compare OPEN SHOP and UNION SHOP.

cloud on title. A claim which, if sustained, would defeat the TITLE of the supposed owner of the property. A judgment, mortgage, or tax lien may constitute a cloud on the title. Compare CLEAR TITLE.

code of law. A collection of written statements of laws; a compilation of laws systematically arranged—for example, the collection of federal tax laws known as the Internal Revenue Code (I.R.C.).

codicil. An addition to a WILL that adds to, subtracts from, revokes, or otherwise changes provisions of the will. It must be executed with the same formalities as a will.

cohabitation. Living together as husband and wife without benefit of clergy.

collapsible corporation. A CORPORATION (defined under the provisions of the Internal Revenue Code, or I.R.C.) formed to manufacture, produce, or purchase property with a view to the disposition of the corporation before the corporation can realize income from its main business. A gain by the stockholders is held to be ordinary income instead of capital gain, even though the gain would have been capital gain if no corporation had been formed.

The I.R.C. denies capital gains treatment to the stockholders if they LIQUIDATE the corporation *in order* to avoid paying ordinary income tax. This is one of the most technical and tricky subjects of tax law.

collateral attack. An attack made against a judgment decision or ruling in some proceeding other than the one in which the judgment decision or ruling is made. A collateral attack is unlike a *direct attack,* which must be made in the same proceeding in which the judgment decision or ruling is made.

collective bargaining. Negotiation between a union and an employer regarding wages, hours, and other conditions of employment, looking toward arriving at a labor agreement. A refusal of either party to bargain is an unfair labor practice under federal law. See LABOR RELATIONS LAW.

collusion. An agreement to perform or carry out some improper or fraudulent plan.

color of title. The appearance of a CLEAR TITLE to property which in fact is a title which may have some defects. Compare UNMARKETABLE TITLE.

combination in restraint of trade. An attempt by two or more persons or corporations to lessen competition by such practices as monopolizing the manufacture or distribution of a product, or controlling prices. Such a combination is unlawful under federal statutes.

comity of states. The practice of a state in recognizing and implementing the laws and court decisions of other states. See FULL FAITH AND CREDIT: This is an extension of a provision in the United States Constitution that "full faith and credit shall be given in each State to the public acts, records, and judicial proceedings of every other State."

commerce. The buying and selling of goods or services. Commerce may be either INTERSTATE or INTRASTATE. INTERSTATE COMMERCE is that referred to in the United States Constitution as "commerce among the several States." Congress is given specific power in the Constitution to regulate interstate commerce. Intrastate commerce is commerce conducted wholly within the boundaries of a particular state. Commerce does not include manufacturing but does include the purchase and sale of commodities, the transportation of persons and property, the use of telephone and telegraph, radio, TV, etc.

An example of interstate commerce is a bus line that runs between New York and Chicago. An example of intrastate commerce is a store in Plains, Georgia, that sells peanuts grown in Georgia. However, a fruit company in Utica, New York, that sells fruit grown and shipped from many different states is engaged in interstate commerce.

One of the most active federal agencies engaged in the regulation of interstate commerce is the INTERSTATE COMMERCE COMMISSION (I.C.C.), which regulates railroads, motor carriers, freight, bus lines, forwarders, and pipelines. The I.C.C. also controls the acquisition, ABANDONMENT, and consolidation of railroads and ferries. It is authorized by Congress to hold hearings and take evidence in cases within its jurisdiction. The final orders of the I.C.C. are reviewable by the federal courts.

Public transportation carriers that operate wholly within a municipality or state are not subject to the jurisdiction of the I.C.C., but are subject to state agencies such as public service commissions.

commercial. Having to do with business. The word is often used in dealing with the buying and selling of merchandise, but in the broad sense it may include all industrial enterprises.

commercial law. That branch of law that governs the rights and relations of persons engaged in COMMERCE or trade. The most comprehensive statutory commercial law is to be found in the Uniform Commercial Code, which prevails in all the states except Louisiana. It governs banking, sales, and nearly every other phase of mercantile and business activity.

commercial paper. See BILLS AND NOTES.

commission merchant. One who receives goods or merchandise to sell. A commission merchant (sometimes called a FACTOR) receives his compensation from the owner of the merchandise sold and the proceeds of the sale. A commission merchant acting as AGENT may sell the merchandise in his own name without disclosing his principal.

commit. To put into legal custody, in a prison or mental institution.

committee. 1. A person or group of persons appointed by a court to act as guardian of the person or property of an INCOMPETENT person. See GUARDIAN.

2. Members of a legislative body who are assigned the responsibility of matters referred to them by the legislature.

common carrier. See CARRIER.

common law. 1. English common law: the body of unwritten law that had developed in England before the American Revolution, much of which was incorporated in the legal systems of the American States. Compare CIVIL LAW.

2. United States common law: principles, usages, and customs as enunciated by the courts of the various states as distinguished from the statutes passed by the legislatures. See CASE LAW and JUDGE-MADE LAW.

common pleas, court of. See COURT.

common stock. See CORPORATION and STOCK.

common-law marriage. A marriage created by agreement instead of a religious or civil ceremony. Only fourteen states now recognize common-law marriages. However, if a couple is "living together" in a common-law state, they may be considered married even if they don't want to be.

common-law maxims. Legal principles expressed in sayings, some of which are derived from Latin phrases. Examples are:

DE MINIMIS *non curat lex.* (The law is not concerned with trifles.)

IGNORANTIA LEGIS NEMINEM EXCUSAT. (Ignorance of the law excuses no one.)

Actions speak louder than words.

A person will not be permitted to do indirectly what he cannot do directly.

The law favors the diligent and the vigilant.

Where two parties are at fault, the law will not aid one as against another.

One should so use his property as not to injure another.

No man should be permitted to profit by his wrongful acts.

For every wrong there is a remedy.

The law looks to the substance and not the form.

community property. According to the laws of eight states, property held by husband and wife jointly.

commutation. The substitution of a lesser penalty than that originally fixed. Such commutation is made by a pardoning power such as a governor of a state or the President.

company. This term is often erroneously used to refer solely to corporations; it may also refer to partnerships or other organizations that carry on business.

comparative negligence. That doctrine of law whereby the NEGLIGENCE of parties to a lawsuit is compared, and proportional recovery is permitted when the negligence of the one suing is less than that of the person sued.

In those states that have adopted this doctrine, the rule of contributory negligence no longer holds.

Example: John Jones is in an automobile accident with Henry Smith, and sues Smith for damages for personal injuries. The jury finds that Jones was 25% to blame for the accident. (Jones suffered a broken arm, from which he made a pretty good recovery.) The jury found that the full amount of Jones' DAMAGES was $4,000. Because Jones' negligence was 25% of the total negligence involved, the jury awarded Jones $3,000.

compensation. 1. The exchange of something of value for property. **2.** The payment of a sum of money as recompense for personal INJURY or property damage.

compensatory damages. See DAMAGES.

competent evidence. See ADMISSIBLE EVIDENCE.

complaint. The first pleading in a lawsuit. Its purpose is to state all the material facts on which the plaintiff relies to support his claim.

composition with creditors. An agreement made between a debtor and his creditors whereby the debtor agrees to pay the creditors a compromise sum in full discharge of his debts.

Example: John Jones owes 35 creditors the total sum of $4000. Jones is faced with bankruptcy. One of his creditors thought the creditors would fare better if Jones stayed out of bankruptcy court. Jones agreed and said he would be willing to pay his creditors $2000 over a period of 2 years provided they agreed not to ask for any interest. All of his creditors agreed, and over a period of 2 years Jones paid his creditors $2,000 in full SATISFACTION of his debts. That was a composition with creditors.

compounding a crime. The agreement for a consideration not to prosecute a crime.

Example: John Jones was a burglar and was caught in the act of burglary by Sam Smith. Jones asked Smith for mercy and said his family was starving. He told Smith he would pay him $500 if Smith would not report or prosecute the burglary. Smith accepted the $500 and did not report or prosecute the burglary. That was compounding a crime (a felony).

compromise and settlement. An agreement between persons to settle their differences and avoid a lawsuit. Note that compromise and settlement is an agreement to be carried out in the future, and is to be distinguished from ACCORD AND SATISFACTION, which is an accomplished fact.

conclusions of law. Determinations made by a judge who tries a case without a jury. The conclusions of law are made at the same time the judge makes findings of fact.

condemnation. The proceeding whereby a government agency takes REAL ESTATE from a private owner without his consent but with an award to the owner to compensate him for the FAIR MARKET VALUE of the property. See EMINENT DOMAIN.

Example: The New York State Highway Department decided to build a new highway between New York City and Utica, New York. The proposed highway went through the middle of John Jones' farm. The New York State Public Works Department tried to purchase a strip of land through Jones' farm, but Jones refused to sell. The Highway Department then brought a proceeding against Jones to *condemn* the strip of land in question. The Highway Department had experts who testified as to the value of the land they sought to condemn. Jones employed his own experts. The New York Court of Claims awarded Jones $2,000 for the land taken for the highway. That was a condemnation proceeding.

condominium. The ownership by various individuals of separate units of a multiunit building (generally an apartment house) and the proportionate ownership or control of the underlying real estate. Although each individual owns a separate unit of the multiunit building, in theory the individual owns the airspace occupied by the separate unit.

A condominium is to be distinguished from an apartment house, which is real estate rented out to various persons, and from a *cooperative* apartment, which is owned by a CORPORATION, the stock of which is held by the tenants.

confession. In criminal law, a statement made by a person charged with a crime in which the person acknowledges guilt. The United States Supreme Court has laid down certain rules which must be followed in order for the confession to be admissible in EVIDENCE.

confession and avoidance. A plea used in civil cases whereby a person sued admits certain facts but alleges new material that nullifies the effect of the material admitted.

> *Example:* John Jones owned a farm on which was located a spring used by his neighbors. One of his neighbors was Howard Brown, to whom Jones refused the privilege of taking water from the spring. Jones brought a court proceeding against Brown, claiming that Brown trespassed on Jones' property to get water from the spring. In the court proceeding, Brown admitted in writing that he trespassed on Jones' land, but said that in 1910 his predecessors in title acquired an EASEMENT to go over this land and an easement to take water from the spring, which easements were transferred to Brown. By admitting the trespass and by setting up new material regarding the easements, Brown pleaded confession and avoidance.

confidential relation. A relationship which exists between client and attorney, principal and agent, trustee and beneficiary, guardian and ward, husband and wife, partners, and others whereby the utmost degree of good faith exists in all transactions between the two. This concept is the basis of *privilege rules*. See EVIDENCE.

conflict of interest. See TRUST.

conflict of laws. That branch of law which determines which jurisdictional law should be given effect and applied to a case involving two jurisdictions. Basically, when a transaction takes place in one state, the courts of another state will recognize the laws of the first state as a matter of COMITY OF STATES or courtesy. Formerly, in contract cases American courts universally applied the law of the place where the contract was made or where the contract was to be performed (called in Latin *lex loci contractus*) as the law of the case being tried. In accident cases American courts would apply the law of the place where the accident took place (called in Latin *lex loci delicti*). In many states the courts now have new rules developed by legal scholars. According to the new rules, the test is *grouping of contacts* or *center of gravity*. That is, courts apply the law of the place which has the most significant relationship to the event and the parties.

Example 1: In the case of *Ingersol* v. *Klein,* the question arose as to whether the law of Illinois or Iowa should govern in an action for wrongful death which resulted from drowning when an automobile being driven in Iowa broke through the ice on the Illinois side of the Mississippi River. All the parties involved in the controversy were residents of Illinois. Technically the accident happened in Iowa, but the court held that the Illinois law should govern because it had the most *significant contacts.*

Example 2: In a lawsuit arising out of an accident which took place in Toronto, Ontario, Canada, the estate of a resident of Quebec, Canada, sued a New York corporation that owned the automobile driven by a New York State resident. The New York law was that of ordinary NEGLIGENCE, while Ontario had a GUEST statute more favorable to the defendants. The New York court applied New York law because New York had more significant contacts in the case than the plaintiff.

A new development relating to conflict of laws has been adopted by many states. This is what is called LONG-ARM STATUTES. The long-arm statute permits a plaintiff who sues in the courts of state X to sue a nonresident defendant who has a place of business in or resides in state Y when it appears that the cause of action arose out of the defendant's activities in state X. The lawbooks are now full of court cases interpreting long-arm statutes.

The general rule has also developed that a person or a corporation in another country or state may be sued for damages where injuries occurred, if that person or corporation has put goods into the stream of INTERSTATE COMMERCE with a probability that goods would come into the state where the person was injured.

confusion of goods. A doctrine of law whereby a person may forfeit his rights to goods he has wrongfully commingled with the goods of another person. The rule has many exceptions and is rarely applied.

consideration. An essential ingredient of every valid contract, it is sometimes referred to as *quid pro quo* for a contractual promise. See *good consideration* and *valuable consideration.*

consortium. The fellowship and basic relationship of a marriage between husband and wife. The word is important because often an action at law is brought not only for personal injury or death of a person but also for *loss of consortium.*

conspiracy. Conspiracy may be of two kinds, civil and criminal. A civil conspiracy is a combination of people who plan to do an unlawful act, not necessarily to commit a CRIME.

Example: Members of a labor union may conspire to break a contract with an employer, or to enter into a secondary boycott. They may be liable for DAMAGES as civil conspirators.

A criminal conspiracy is a combination of two or more persons who plan to accomplish (but who do not necessarily carry out) some criminal act, or some lawful act by criminal means.

Example: A group of people may formulate a plan to set fire to an old building they own and thus collect insurance. That would be a criminal conspiracy. Any plan by a group of people to blackmail or extort money, to fraudulently use the mails, to interfere with civil rights, to pervert or hinder justice, or to prevent persons from working by force or intimidation may constitute criminal conspiracy.

Prosecutors generally prefer to try cases for criminal conspiracy rather than for the crime itself, because it is usually easier to prove conspiracy.

constable. An officer in a town or other municipality responsible for maintaining public order or performing civil duties assigned by a court.

constitutional law. That branch of law which deals with the organization and powers of government. Although each of the 50 states has a constitution, and state courts are continually interpreting and defining state constitution powers and obligations, the bulk of constitutional law deals with the United States Constitution as construed and interpreted by the United States Supreme Court. Constitutional law concerns itself with every phase of daily living, including freedom of speech, freedom of the press, freedom of assembly, freedom of religion, equal protection of laws, and due process of law.

Constitutional law concerns itself with practically every branch of government. The government of the United States is unique in its separation of powers into three branches: the legislative branch, the executive branch, and the judicial branch. (That separation of powers is true not only in the case of the national government but also in every state in the nation.) No one of the three branches of government may constitutionally encroach on the powers of another branch.

When the Constitution was written in 1787, its framers did not feel that a Bill of Rights was a necessary part of a federal constitution. Some of the delegates, however, insisted on a Bill of Rights, and eventually this took the form of the first ten Amendments to the Constitution.

Rights granted by the First Amendment ("First Amendment rights") are freedom of religion, FREEDOM OF SPEECH AND OF THE PRESS, and the right of peaceable assembly. The United States Supreme Court has written volumes of millions of words interpreting those rights. What, for example, does freedom of speech mean? Can a person use obscene language in public with impunity? The Court generally has been lenient toward obscene language (see OBSCENITY), but has put other restrictions on free speech. Justice Oliver Wendell Holmes pointed out that free speech does not permit a person to cry "Fire" in a crowded theater or by the exercise of free speech to start a run on a bank.

DUE PROCESS OF LAW is a subject which all American courts, including the Supreme Court, have concerned themselves with in thousands of court cases. Although the term does not have a well-defined meaning, it does mean that the government must not be arbitrary in its exercise of power and must exercise established rules for the security of private rights which involve liberty or property.

In 1868 the Fourteenth Amendment to the Constitution was ratified. This Amendment prohibits the states from making any law which deprives any person of "life, liberty, or property" without due process of law or which denies to any person equal protection of laws.

Constitutional law deserves a lifetime of study. Times change, as does the makeup of the federal courts which interpret the Constitution, and the Constitution is interpreted in broader or narrower ways. Some people contend that many of the Supreme Court's decisions when Earl Warren was Chief Justice were revolutionary, but we have survived and are now living in a new era under the guidance of the so-called Burger Court. The amazing thing is that the American people of whatever party or opinion usually accept decisions of the Supreme Court as the final word of law in this country.

construction proceeding. See WILL.

constructive eviction. A disturbance of a tenant's possessions by a landlord, or conditions which the landlord permits, whereby the leased premises are rendered UNTENANTABLE—unfit or unsuitable for occupancy.

consumer protection laws. Legislation passed by Congress and most states to protect the interests and rights of the consuming public. There are many federal laws dealing with consumer protection, and all the states have enacted laws to protect consumers against unfair and deceptive practices. Among the practices that are forbidden or regulated are low-price traps, phony home-improvement schemes, automobile insurance frauds, missing-heir schemes, door-to-door sales, the sending of unsolicited merchandise, referral sales, and false and misleading advertising. See also BLUE-SKY LAWS.

contempt of court. Contempt of court may be civil or criminal. A civil contempt is the doing or failure to do something which a court has ordered done outside the courtroom for the benefit of a party to a legal proceeding.

Example: A court issues an injunction forbidding John Doe to cross a certain bridge on the property of Samuel Roe. Doe ignores the court's order and crosses the bridge to the property of Roe. John Doe is guilty of civil contempt of court.

A criminal contempt of court is an act done in disrespect or disobedience in the presence of the court which obstructs the administration of justice.

Example: John Smith is being tried in Judge Brown's court. Smith uses insulting language to Judge Brown. Smith probably would be held guilty of criminal contempt of court and subject to punishment by Judge Brown.

contest of a will. See WILL CONTEST.

contingent. Depending on an event the occurrence of which is uncertain.

contingent fee. An amount payable to someone (generally a lawyer) dependent on the outcome of a lawsuit. Also called a *contingency fee.*

contingent liability. A LIABILITY that depends on an uncertain event, as opposed to a liability that is fixed or certain. A contingent liability may become an absolute liability upon the happening of a certain event.

Example: A guarantor of a lease agrees to pay rent to the landlord if the tenant becomes bankrupt. Under such a guarantee the liability of the guarantor is contingent. If the tenant becomes bankrupt, the liability of the guarantor becomes absolute.

continuance. The postponement of a legal PROCEEDING.

Example: John Jones and Samuel Smith are about to engage in the trial of a civil lawsuit. One of Jones' principal witnesses is stricken with pneumonia. Jones' lawyer asks for a continuance of the case until the witness recovers from pneumonia. The court grants the continuance.

contract. An agreement between two or more persons or parties. Legally, a contract involves an offer and an acceptance and should be supported by CONSIDERATION. A contract is generally in writing, as a document that expresses the agreement between the parties.

Example: John Jones owns a house and lot on Mayberry Drive. He enters into a legal agreement with Howard Smith to sell his house and lot on Mayberry Drive for $35,000. The parties have entered into a contract.

A contract may be express or implied. An *express contract* is one stated in explicit and distinct language.

Example: John Jones enters into a written agreement with Sam Smith to purchase 35 bushels of wheat at $3 a bushel, to be delivered by Smith to Jones on the first of March.

An *implied contract* is one inferred by law as a matter of reason and justice, and/or is implied from the acts or conduct of the parties and the circumstances surrounding the transaction.

Example: Joe Brown registers at the Imperial Hotel and inquires of the desk clerk how much the daily charge is for one room. The clerk says $50 a day. Brown takes the room and stays a week. He has made an implied contract to pay the hotel $50 a day for the occupancy of the room.

Some contracts have to be in writing. These include (a) contracts to convey real estate; (b) contracts of guarantee; (c) contracts not to be performed within 1 year; (d) contracts for the sale of goods in excess of a stated dollar amount (depending on the law of a particular state). The failure of one party to perform a contractual obligation may result in a court action for BREACH OF CONTRACT.

contributory negligence. See NEGLIGENCE.

conversion. 1. The equitable exchange of one form of property for another (as real estate for personal property or personal property for real estate) to carry out some just and equitable purpose. **2.** A wrongful and unauthorized assumption and exercise of the right of ownership of goods or personal chattels belonging to another. A wrongful INTENT is not an essential element of this type of conversion. It is sufficient if the owner of the goods or chattels has been deprived of his property or possessions by someone's unauthorized act in assuming dominion and control over the property.

conveyance. A TRANSFER of TITLE to real property.

cooperative apartment. See CONDOMINIUM.

copyright law. A copyright is the registration of the owner's right to print, publish, or sell a literary, dramatic, musical, artistic, or similar work. A United States copyright law was enacted in 1976 (effective January 1, 1978) which superseded the copyright law of 1909. The old law protected the owner of a copyright for 28 years from the date of the first publication and could be renewed for a second period of 28 more years. For literary, artistic, dramatic, musical and similar works created *after* January 1, 1978, the new law provides protection during the author's lifetime plus an additional period of protection to his heirs of 50 years after his death. The 1978 law also makes a number of significant changes in the copyright system.

Except in limited circumstances, copyrighted material may not be reproduced without the permission of the copyright holder.

coram nobis. An ancient WRIT which has been revived in recent years. It is a court review of previous criminal court proceedings to determine whether an ERROR has been committed in the previous proceedings. See CERTIORARI and JUDICIAL REVIEW.

corespondent. See DIVORCE.

coroner. A public official, usually a medical doctor, whose duties include inquiry into any death that seems unexplained by natural causes, and in most states into deaths where no doctor was in attendance. A coroner is also called a *medical examiner.*

corporation. An artificial "person" created by the legislature. In the early days of the United States, every corporation was created by an act of the legislature. Then the corporation laws of the various states were changed so that a corporation could be created by the filing with the state of certain papers such as a corporate CHARTER defining the powers and authority of the corporation. A corporation is owned by its STOCKHOLDERS. The stockholders elect DIRECTORS, who have the responsibility of the corporation's overall management. The directors in turn appoint officers and agents, who engage in the day-to-day management of the corporation.

There are various kinds of STOCK of a corporation: *common stock* entitles the owner to a pro rata share of the profits of the corporation if a DIVIDEND is declared; *preferred stock* gives its owners precedence over the owners of the common stock in the payment of dividends or in the distribution of the assets of the corporation in the event of its dissolution; *par stock* bears a face value; *no-par stock* has no cash PAR VALUE but simply entitles the owners to a proportionate interest in the assets of the corporation.

corpus delicti. Literally, this Latin phrase means "body of the crime." It is a doctrine holding that before a person accused of a crime can be held or otherwise detained, there must be substantial proof before the court that a crime has been committed.

> *Example:* A famous murder was said to have been committed when a man took a girl on a lake in a rowboat. He was alleged to have strangled the girl and then to have tied her body with his trousers and thrown her overboard. The body was never found. The man was arrested for murder. He was brought before a judge, who freed him from the murder charge because there was no *corpus delicti.*

counsel (counsellor). These words mean, and are often used interchangeably with, the words "lawyer" and "attorney-at-law." Sometimes a lawyer who is associated with another lawyer for the purpose of either advising or arguing the case in court is referred to as OF COUNSEL.

count. A statement of CAUSE OF ACTION. Generally where several causes of action are stated in one complaint, each statement is known as a count.

counterclaim. A claim stated in opposition to a claim in a lawsuit. A counterclaim must tend to reduce the *plaintiff*'s demand and generally must arise out of the same transaction pleaded by the plaintiff.

county. An administrative division of a state.

course of employment. See IN THE COURSE OF.

court. The variety of difference in the laws of the 50 states and the federal government are no better illustrated than in the American court system. Basically, courts are those of *original jurisdiction* (where a court case is first brought) and *appellate courts* (where cases are taken for JUDICIAL REVIEW). Courts may also be classified as *courts of record* and *courts not of record.* A court of record is one that keeps permanent records of its PROCEEDINGS and has power to fine or imprison a person; a court not of record is an inferior court that has no power to fine or imprison and does not keep permanent records of its proceedings.

Courts of original or general jurisdiction may be called in some states *superior courts,* in some states *courts of common pleas,* and in some states *district courts.*

Most states call their highest appellate courts *supreme courts.* To maintain its individuality, New York State calls its highest appellate court the Court of Appeals.

The United States Constitution provides that "The judicial power of the United States, shall be vested in one Supreme Court, and in such inferior courts as Congress may from time to time ordain and establish." Congress has ordained and established 10 court of appeals, 89 federal district courts, and one Court of Claims, which hears suits against the government.

Federal courts have jurisdiction over suits between citizens of different states (see DIVERSITY OF CITIZENSHIP) when the amount involved is at least $10,000, or between a state and an alien; a suit involving a question arising under the Constitution or the laws of the United States (called a federal question); and in ADMIRALTY, BANKRUPTCY, PATENT, COPYRIGHT, postal, INTERNAL REVENUE, and most LABOR RELATIONS matters.

court costs. Sometimes referred to as "costs." Certain amounts fixed by statute, supposedly to reimburse a successful party in an action or special proceeding for expenses arising out of the suit. Unfortunately, costs generally do not reimburse the successful party for all legal expenses.

> *Example:* Mary Jones has Robert Smith, a lawyer, sue George Brown for damages because of injuries sustained by Jones in an auto accident involving cars driven by Jones and Brown. Jones won the case by proving that Brown was to blame for the accident. The jury awarded a verdict in her favor for $3500. Jones' lawyer, who spent 21 hours preparing the case for trial and 3 days in court trying the case, charged her $975 for legal services. She was able to add to the jury's verdict the sum of $175 in court costs, which was grossly inadequate to reimburse her for her legal expenses.

court order. See ORDER.

court reporter. See TRIAL.

court-martial. A military court, generally composed of military or naval officers and convened by military authority to try a member of the armed forces or someone under military jurisdiction.

covenant. A formal agreement in writing whereby one of the parties pledges to do certain things or stipulates as to the truth of certain facts. Sometimes a deed of real estate is called a *full covenant* deed. That is because the deed may contain a number of covenants, such as a *covenant for peaceful enjoyment,* a *covenant of title,* etc.

credibility. Generally, believability of WITNESSES. The question of credibility is usually submitted by a judge to a jury when he tells them that the jury is the sole judge of the facts, and that they may pass on the weight and credibility of the testimony of every witness. Credibility may depend on such circumstances as the appearance of witnesses on the witness stand, their manner, the way they answer questions, their hesitancy or evasiveness, or their seeming candor.

crime. An act in violation of the criminal laws of a state or nation; an offense against the people of the state. A crime may be either a FELONY (punishable by imprisonment in a penitentiary or in some instances by execution) or a lesser crime called a MISDEMEANOR.

criminal law. That branch of law which deals with crimes and their punishment.

cross-examination. The questioning of a WITNESS, after DIRECT EXAMINATION, during a TRIAL or at a pretrial hearing by the lawyer for the opposition party. The purpose of cross-examination is to test or discredit the witness. The opposition lawyer usually may not ask questions on subjects not introduced during direct examination.

cum testamento annexo **(C.T.A.).** "With the will annexed"—sometimes applied when the EXECUTOR named in a will is dead or unable to act and the court appoints an administrator not named in the will to administer it.

curtesy. The life interest of a widower in his wife's real estate after her death. Curtesy exists only if there are offspring from the marriage living at the time of the wife's death. The right of curtesy has been abolished by most American states.

custodia legis. "Custody of the law," which a legal officer acting in his official capacity has over specified property.

cy pres. **1.** A doctrine that when it is impossible to carry out exactly a provision of the will, the intention of the testator should be carried out as closely as possible (the term comes from old French for "so near"). **2.** A will providing for a charitable bequest or devise that cannot be legally accomplished with exactness.

D

damages. Compensation for an INJURY or a loss. The amount of damages may be determined by a judge or by a jury. When a person sues for damages, the party who sues is called the PLAINTIFF and the party being sued is called the DEFENDANT.

Damages are of various kinds or classes: *compensatory damages* are awarded as compensation for the loss sustained by the plaintiff; *punitive damages* (sometimes called smart money) are awarded in addition to compensatory damages as punishment or to make an example of the defendant; *general damages* are those which ordinarily result from the wrong complained of, such as an auto repair results from an auto accident; *liquidated damages* are agreed on by the parties beforehand or made part of a contract, a breach of which results in damages; *special damages* are the amount claimed by the person injured to cover loss of wages, medical bills, etc.

In personal injury cases, the injured person's damages as determined by a judge or jury may take into consideration the plaintiff's PAIN AND SUFFERING, the extent of the injuries, the personal insult and indignity caused by the injuries, and such amount of money as the judge or jury may find to be just and proper compensation for the injury.

In determining the amount of damages to personal property such as an automobile, either of two methods of proof may be used. One method, generally used when there is a total loss of property, is to determine the difference between the reasonable and FAIR MARKET VALUE of the property before and after the accident. The other method is to determine the reasonable and fair cost of repairs necessary to put the property in as good condition as it was before the accident.

damnum absque injuria. A phrase meaning that damage has been sustained without INJURY in the legal sense. Such a loss, for which there is no legal recovery, occurs rather rarely.

date of issue. Generally the date when a defendant files an answer to a complaint; in other words, the date when ISSUE has been joined.

de bonis non. A Latin phrase meaning "of goods not . . ." often used when an administrator of an estate is appointed to succeed another who had partially administered the estate. The new administrator is granted "letters of administration *de bonis non*," meaning that he is administrator of that portion of the estate which has not been settled.

de facto. Actually existing in fact but without a legal basis. It may refer to a government or a CORPORATION. For example, a dictator may establish a *de facto* government without lawful title.

de jure. Legitimate and lawful, thus differing from DE FACTO. For example, a CORPORATION which has complied with all legal requirements under state laws may be a *de jure* corporation; whereas a corporation *de facto* may have all the appearances of a corporation and exercise all the powers of a corporation, but without having proper legal authority to so act.

de minimis. **1.** Frivolous. **2.** Not of sufficient importance to warrant legal action. See COMMON-LAW MAXIMS.

de novo. A Latin phrase meaning "anew" or "with a fresh start."

> *Example:* I once had a motion for a NEW TRIAL before a judge who delighted in using Latin. When the lawyers for both sides appeared at the judge's office, I began by saying that I knew the judge had reviewed many cases since our case was tried and therefore I would briefly review the facts of the case. The judge said, "I agree. We will review this case *de novo*"—that is, review it with a fresh start.

de son tort. A French phrase meaning "of his own wrong." A person who takes upon himself to act in a legal capacity without legal authority acts of his own wrong, or *de son tort.*

death penalty. See CAPITAL CRIME.

debenture (debenture bond). A BOND that is unsecured by particular assets and is payable out of a CORPORATION's earnings and general assets. It is to be distinguished from a MORTGAGE bond, which is a LIEN on land held by the corporation.

decedent. A person who has died. Very often in estate parlance the decedent is the person whose estate is being administered. In actions for wrongful death, the decedent is the one who was killed in an accident.

decision on the merits. A decision that determines basically the right and wrong of the litigation. Sometimes a court decides a case on technical grounds, such as the fact that the court does not have jurisdiction of the action; such a decision is not a decision on the merits.

declaration. In a lawsuit, a statement of the facts and circumstances constituting the complainant's CAUSE OF ACTION. It is sometimes called the
COMPLAINT and may be the first of a series of pleadings in a lawsuit.

declaratory judgment. A JUDGMENT that states the rights of the parties but
does not order or direct any person to do anything. Asking for a declaratory judgment is a relatively recent development of the law.

> *Example:* The Excelsior Insurance Company insured A for a liability
> arising out of the operation of a Buick auto. The policy provided that
> the company should not be responsible for damages if the Buick was
> used for hire. At the time of the particular accident when B was
> injured, according to the version of the Excelsior Insurance Com-
> pany, the Buick was being used as a taxicab, and the insurance com-
> pany said there was no coverage. B sued A, making a claim against
> A for $10,000 damages, saying that he was injured as the result of an
> automobile accident involving the Buick. Should the Excelsior Com-
> pany defend the suit or attempt to settle B's claim? To answer that
> question, the Excelsior Company brought a court action seeking a
> declaratory judgment, which would state whether or not the company
> was responsible for any damages which B may have sustained as a
> result of the accident and whether or not the company had an obliga-
> tion to defend the suit. If they did not bring an action for a declara-
> tory judgment, the insurance company would be subjecting itself to
> the expense of defending the lawsuit or, if it did not defend the law-
> suit, it would be running the risk of having a large verdict rendered
> for B against A, for the payment of which A might sue the insurance
> company. The insurance company eliminated the risk of subjecting
> itself to liability by bringing the action for declaratory judgment.

decree. 1. A decision of a government authority. **2.** A JUDGMENT or order
of a court.

dedication. Transfer of TITLE to land to the public, with the understanding
that a public authority will put the land to public use.

> *Example:* John Doe owned a large tract of land used informally by
> children as a baseball and football field. He dedicated the land to the
> City of Bellville with the understanding that the city would improve
> the land and use it as a public playground.

deduction. In TAX law, an item subtracted from a person's gross income in
arriving at net taxable income.

deed. In REAL ESTATE law, a written instrument that conveys TITLE to real
estate. The essentials of such a deed are (a) the parties, who are known
as the grantor (the one who conveys the land) and the grantee (the one
to whom the land is conveyed); (b) a description of the land conveyed;

(c) the CONSIDERATION for the deed, which may be the actual money paid for the land or may simply recite "for love and affection" or "one dollar and other good and valuable consideration" (sometimes referred to as "$1.00 and o.g. + v.c."); (d) words of conveyance, such as "grant and convey"; (e) the signature of the grantor acknowledged or witnessed; and (f) the DELIVERY of the deed to the grantee. So far as the public or third persons are concerned, the deed should be recorded in a public office, but as between the grantor and grantee a deed does not have to be recorded.

There are various forms of deeds that have different legal effects. A QUITCLAIM DEED is one in which the grantor does not guarantee legal title to the property conveyed. A *bargain and sale deed* is almost the same as a quitclaim deed except that the grantor guarantees that he has done nothing to encumber the property or adversely affect the title since he acquired the property. A WARRANTY *deed* is a deed whereby the grantor guarantees or warrants the validity of the title to the land. A *full covenant deed* is a slightly stronger form of warranty deed.

deed to secure debts. See MORTGAGE.

defamation. Injuring another person's good name and reputation. A person who defames another without good cause may be liable in damages for LIBEL AND SLANDER.

default. In general, a failure to do something which one is obligated to do. The term may arise in the case of a contract when a person fails to do what the contract requires him to do. Or it may refer to the failure to take some action in a legal proceeding, such as the failure of a defendant to answer or appear in court.

default judgment. A JUDGMENT entered without the defendant's being heard in his own defense, by reason of either his failure to file an answer to the complaint or his failure to appear at the trial.

defeasance. A legal INSTRUMENT that terminates the force and effect of some other legal act or DEED.

defect of parties. Whenever a lawsuit is instituted, the plaintiff has to sue the proper parties. If, when a suit is instituted, there is failure or omission in the parties brought in to solve the legal controversy, such a failure or omission is a defect of parties.

defective title. A TITLE to personal property or real estate which is not legal or good. See UNMARKETABLE TITLE.

defendant. A person against whom a legal proceeding is brought in a civil or criminal court. In a civil case he is sued; in a criminal case he is accused of a crime.

defensive allegation. A settlement in answer of a defendant in a civil proceeding, either denying the sufficiency of a complaint or alleging new facts that may constitute a defense in the lawsuit.

dehors. A French word meaning "outside." In legal parlance it may mean "foreign to" or "unconnected with"—for example, an AMICUS CURIAE is *dehors* a case in which it files a brief.

del credere agent. A FACTOR who agrees to pay his principal the price of the goods sold by him if the purchaser does not pay—who in other words guarantees the payment of the purchase price of goods sold by him. (From the Italian, "of trust.")

delivery. The final act whereby a right is transferred to another person. In the case of a contract, lease, or deed the parties may have signed the document, but it is not effective until it is physically handed over.

demand. A claim for something due. The word may have special meaning in law. Sometimes a demand for the payment of money or the performance of an act may be a prerequisite to some legal right such as the right to sue.

> *Example:* John Doe lends his tractor to his neighbor, Sam Smith. Smith fails to return the tractor within a reasonable time. Doe may sue Smith for the return of his tractor, but first he should make a demand in writing for the return of the tractor.

demand note. A PROMISSORY NOTE payable immediately or ON DEMAND.

demise. 1. In REAL ESTATE law, a lease or conveyance to some person of land for life or a term of years. **2.** Death.

demurrer. An application to the court to dismiss a pleading because of *insufficiency*—that is, a claim that even if the allegations were true, they would not constitute sufficient grounds for the proceeding.

deponent. A person who gives evidence under oath or who makes an AFFIDAVIT.

deportation. The sending back of an alien to his native country. When immigration officials determine that an alien should be deported, the Attorney General may issue a warrant for the alien's arrest. The alien will then go before a special hearing officer appointed by the Attorney General. The alien has the right to be represented by counsel at the hearing. All precautions are taken to insure that the alien is treated fairly. A person may be deported for illegal entry into the United States, for overstaying the specified time limit, for becoming a public charge, for prostitution or other immoral practices, for subversive activities, for criminal conduct, etc.

deposition. Legal TESTIMONY taken under oath, with the WITNESS subject to CROSS-EXAMINATION and the testimony transcribed by a stenographer. Generally a deposition takes place before the actual trial of a legal action. The grounds for taking a pretrial deposition are many. The witness whose testimony is taken by deposition may not be able to be present at the trial. The deposition may be a means to discover facts needed for the trial. Or the purpose of the deposition may be to perpetuate testimony which might otherwise be lost. A few years ago lawyers used to object to pretrial depositions as "fishing expeditions." Now most lawyers favor them as part of the "race" for disclosure of facts, and most states are liberal in allowing them.

deposits in court. Money deposited in court to safeguard it until it can be legally determined who is entitled to it. Sometimes a person holds money claimed by two or more other people. The person pays the money into court until the court determines which claimant or claimants own the money.

  The law of the particular state designates what custodian shall hold the money deposited in court, and whether interest shall be paid on the money pending its disposition.

depreciation. A lessening of value of an asset. In TAX law, the rate or percentage of deductible depreciation may have considerable significance.

deputy. A substitute; a person who acts in the place of the person for whom he is deputy.

  Example: A deputy sheriff is one appointed to act in the place of the sheriff when the latter is unavailable.

descent and distribution. The rules of descent and distribution are the rules for the inheritance of the property of a person who dies INTESTATE. Descent refers to the inheritance of real estate, and distribution refers to the inheritance of personal property. These rules are enacted by each state. Such legislation stipulates the fractional interest inherited by spouse, descendants, ascendants, brothers and sisters, uncles, aunts, cousins, etc. (It is surprising how the laws of the 50 states differ on the subject.)

desegregation. The elimination of separation of races. It took nearly 100 years after the Civil War for the United States Supreme Court to hold that racial segregation in public schools and facilities was unconstitutional. In the 1950s the Supreme Court, in a number of decisions, banned such segregation and ordered that segregation practices be stopped. However, because the country is so large and complex, the Court ordered that desegregation be carried out under the supervision of the U.S. District Courts. See CIVIL RIGHTS.

destitute. Without the necessities of life; in the condition of want.

determination. Generally the end or termination of a lawsuit. It may be accomplished by the JUDGMENT of a court or judge or by the act of the parties to the suit (such as a DISCONTINUANCE).

detinue. A COMMON-LAW action for the recovery of specific property. This form of action has been largely superseded in the law of most American states by lawsuits such as REPLEVIN.

devastavit. A Latin word that literally means "it has wasted"; a term formerly in general use to mean misapplication or wasting of the assets of an estate.

devise. A gift by WILL of real estate. It should not be confused with a BEQUEST, which is a gift by will of personal property or money. (The distinction between "devise" and "bequest" has been abolished by some states.) A *devisee* is the person to whom real estate is given by will.

dictum (sometimes *obiter dictum*). Something which is said by a judge in a decision in the nature of an observation on a case, but which isn't necessary for the determination of a court ruling.

dilatory plea. A tactic, used by a defendant in a lawsuit, not going to the merits of the case but specifically for delay purposes.

diligence. In law, CARE exercised by a person. The word is often used with the word "due": *due diligence* means the appropriate use of care or diligence under particular circumstances.

direct attack. See COLLATERAL ATTACK.

direct examination. When a WITNESS is called to the witness stand, the party who calls the witness asks questions to bring out the witness' story. These questions are direct examination, or sometimes *examination in chief*. Compare CROSS-EXAMINATION.

directed verdict. A VERDICT that a judge directs a jury to make in a civil case in which the EVIDENCE is overwhelmingly in favor of one party.

director. A word generally used to indicate a member of a board of directors that manages a CORPORATION or similar organization.

disability. In law, inability to work. There are various degrees of disability, including permanent disability; total permanent disability; temporary disability; and partial disability (permanent or temporary). The various degrees of disability become most important in personal injury and WORKMEN'S COMPENSATION cases. See WHOLLY AND PERMANENTLY DISABLED.

disbarment. Rescinding a lawyer's license to practice law by reason of illegal or unethical conduct. It is usually done by a state court initiated by a state BAR ASSOCIATION.

discharge. 1. To cancel an obligation. **2.** To release a person from any debt owed. In contract law, when a person fulfills his obligations to a contract, he has discharged those obligations. **3.** In BANKRUPTCY LAW, after a person files a petition in bankruptcy and fulfills certain formalities, he may be released from the obligation of all his debts. He has been *discharged in bankruptcy.* **4.** A person who accepts the money or property due him from the assets of the estate of a deceased person may discharge the estate from further obligation.

discontinue. To terminate or put an end to a legal PROCEEDING. Legal proceedings may be discontinued by the written stipulation of the attorneys, by court order, or by abandonment of the proceeding by the person who instituted it.

discovered negligence doctrine. See LAST CLEAR CHANCE.

discovery. The disclosure of EVIDENCE, facts, and documents, relative to the prosecution or defense of a lawsuit. The most notable improvement and modernization of legal procedure during the past half century has been in the field of discovery. In former times there was such a thing in legal practice, but it was circumscribed with technicalities; so that finding out all the facts on the other side of a lawsuit was very difficult and complicated. Today anybody connected with a lawsuit may be subject to oral examination regarding any relevant fact in the case; books and papers must be produced for examination; and facts so discovered have to be admitted as evidence.

discretion. Individual judgment. The word is used in many branches of law. For example, in the trial of a lawsuit a judge in his judicial discretion may grant certain RELIEF and an appellate court will not interfere with the exercise of that discretion. (But see ABUSE OF DISCRETION.) Other matters involving the exercise of discretion include the case of a trustee who is called upon to make certain investments or to decide whether or not to invade the principal of a TRUST for the trust's beneficiary. In the exercise of discretion a person has to decide what is right and proper under certain circumstances, and he must often use good judgment as well as courage. See PRUDENT MAN RULE.

discrimination. Unequal treatment. The law says that all persons shall be treated equally. Discrimination in areas covered by law is illegal. At one time more was heard of discrimination in connection with railways that were supposed to treat all shippers alike. Some railroads favored some shippers against others and were thereby guilty of discrimination. Now we hear more of discrimination against black people and women in employment and other matters. See CIVIL RIGHTS.

disinherit. To cut off or deprive a person of his interest in an estate when he would otherwise, according to state laws, inherit property.

> *Example:* Years ago there was a famous case of a wealthy man who by his will wished to disinherit one of his sons. To that son by his will he gave nothing but a pair of cufflinks. The point of that clause of disinheritance was to show that the disinheritance was not a mistake or a case of forgetfulness. The father by bequeathing his son a pair of cufflinks demonstrated that he knew that son was alive and capable of receiving a gift.

dismiss. To put an end to a lawsuit or legal proceeding. Generally a lawsuit is dismissed by a judgment of the court or a stipulation of DISCONTINUANCE signed by the attorneys in the lawsuit. In some states the term signifies the withdrawal of a lawsuit or other legal proceeding. Of course, if a party to the suit wishes to withdraw or discontinue a court action after it has proceeded to an advanced stage, he may have to pay COURT COSTS incurred by the other side up to that point. If, before submission to a jury, a case is dismissed by a judge because of insufficiency at law, that dismissal is called a *nonsuit.*

dismissal without prejudice. See WITH PREJUDICE, WITHOUT PREJUDICE.

disorderly conduct. Public acts that disturb the peace or endanger community morals, health, or safety. Often disorderly conduct is a catch phrase to denote an offense when the arresting officer is uncertain as to whether or not some other crime has been committed.

dispossess. To oust a person from real estate by legal proceedings. A *dispossess proceeding* is a statutory proceeding whereby a landlord can get rid of a tenant for nonpayment of rent or other breach of the lease. Dispossession of a tenant is also known as eviction.

dissolution. A breaking up or termination. It may occur in several legal situations. In the case of a CONTRACT, a dissolution is the cancellation of the contract by the parties to it. A CORPORATION may be dissolved when its existence is terminated by either voluntary dissolution on the part of the STOCKHOLDERS or involuntary dissolution by the state in which the corporation is incorporated. A marriage may be said to be dissolved when it is terminated by DIVORCE or ANNULMENT.

distrain. To hold property of another as a pledge or security for the performance of some obligation.

district attorney. The prosecuting attorney for a judicial district. He has broad powers and wide discretion in determining what crimes should be prosecuted and what individuals should be charged with crime.

district court. See COURT.

disturbance of the peace. See BREACH OF THE PEACE.

diversity of citizenship. In federal law, jurisdiction over a controversy is held by a federal court if the suit is brought between citizens of different states or between a U.S. citizen and an alien. This situation is called diversity of citizenship or *diversity jurisdiction*.

dividend. Broadly speaking, the division of a fund among several people. The most common use of the word is in connection with CORPORATIONS. A *corporate dividend* is a payment to its STOCKHOLDERS by a corporation out of its profits and assets.

There are various types of dividends. A LIQUIDATING DIVIDEND may be a partial return of the capital to stockholders of a corporation that is going out of business. *Stock dividends* are paid in stock of the corporation rather than in cash.

In BANKRUPTCY LAWS a dividend may be the amount divided *pro rata* between creditors of a bankrupt estate.

divorce. A legal action that completely breaks the bonds of marriage. The legislature of each state has the right to prescribe the grounds for divorce. The basic grounds standard in most of the 50 states are: ADULTERY, conviction of a crime, mental or physical cruelty, habitual drunkenness, habitual use of drugs, INCOMPATIBILITY, insanity, impotence, personal indignities, nonsupport, loathsome disease, vagrancy, and venereal disease. In recent years many states have eliminated some of these grounds and have substituted or added NO-FAULT grounds, which makes the granting of divorce relatively simple. For example, a number of states have provided that an *irretrievable breakdown* of the marriage is grounds for divorce. Even in such divorces, however, many legal problems may remain, such as the custody of children, alimony, and disposition of property owned by the parties to the marriage. In the days when adultery was the popular ground of divorce, generally the suit papers named an outside person as the person with whom the defendant had adulterous relationship. Such outside person was known as a *corespondent*. Today corespondents are seldom named because of the prevalence of no-fault divorces.

divorce a vinculo. See MENSA ET THORO.

docket. A court record of PROCEEDINGS. Some law offices have dockets that list all pending litigated matters in the office.

Doe, John (Jane). A fictitious name used when the real party to a transaction is undisclosed or unknown. The name may also be used in a hypothetical illustration given to state a legal principle.

doing business. A phrase that legally may be most important in cases of out-of-state or foreign corporations to determine whether or not they are subject to state taxation, whether they are subject to state regulation, or whether they can be sued. Most states tax foreign corporations that are doing business within that state. Volumes have been written on the subject by courts deciding whether or not a foreign corporation is doing business within a particular state. Generally, the transaction of a single piece of business does not constitute "doing business." The question is a constitutional one, because corporations that are simply transacting business all through the United States and engaged in INTERSTATE COMMERCE are not doing business in a particular state.

domestic relations court. See FAMILY COURT.

domicile. A person's permanent place of residence and a place to which, when he is absent, he returns or plans to return. A domicile is distinguished from a residence, which may be only temporary. Domicile is residency with the intent to stay there permanently.

> *Example:* John Smith has his permanent home at 72nd Street in New York City, his summer home is in Newport, Rhode Island, and a winter residence is in Colorado, where he skis. New York City is his domicile.

donee. In the law of wills, when a POWER OF APPOINTMENT is given, the person who is given it is called the donee. A donor is the giver of a gift, or the person who creates a power of appointment.

double indemnity. A provision in a life insurance policy for double payment of the face value of the policy in the event that the insured dies because of an accident.

double jeopardy. Putting a person on trial for an offense that he has previously been tried for if the first trial had gone to a conclusion. It is a sacred principle of American law that no person shall be put in double jeopardy. This rule was incorporated in the Fifth Amendment to the Constitution of the United States, which reads, "No person shall . . . be subject for the same offense to be twice put in jeopardy of life or limb." The same principle appears in most state constitutions.

Of course you may say, "What does that mean? Why should a person be tried twice for the same offense?" In the history of our nation there have been countless cases where a person once tried for an offense is arrested for a second time. Sometimes a number of offenses arise out of the same criminal act or a sequence of criminal acts. It may be a highly technical matter to determine if the person is being tried for several crimes or being tried for the same crime several times and thus put in double jeopardy. The prohibition against double jeopardy means that once a trial is over, the prosecutor may not look for new evidence of the *same* crime and seek to reopen the case.

dower. A widow's right to a life interest in, usually, one third of her husband's real estate. The fraction may vary from state to state.

down payment. See EARNEST MONEY and BINDER.

draft. 1. A bill of exchange in the law of negotiable INSTRUMENTS. **2.** Military conscription. **3.** The preparation of a legal instrument or legislative bill.

drugs and narcotics laws. The area of drugs and narcotics is a most important field of law. Although the laws of the 50 states govern some phases of the problem, the major part of the field is preempted by the federal Food and Drug Administration (F.D.A.), which carries out the provisions of the Federal Food, Drug, and Cosmetics Act. The F.D.A. regulates the manufacture, distribution, and sale of drugs, cosmetics, and narcotics. A drug is generally defined as a medicine for the treatment of human diseases; that is, a medicine for both internal and external use. A *proprietary drug* is one that is packaged and sold over the counter to the public. A *prescription drug* is one that may be sold only on the written order of a physician. A narcotic may sometimes be a medicine, but when used in large doses may produce poisonous effects such as stupor or convulsions. Both state and federal laws attempt to control narcotics, but the traffic in narcotics is heavy and profitable, and the problem is difficult.

due care. Legally, the sufficient CARE that a prudent person would exercise under certain circumstances.

due process of law. Basically, this means legal proceedings that are fair and follow established procedures. The phrase may, however, mean different things under different circumstances. The Fifth Amendment to the U.S. Constitution says no person shall "be deprived of life, liberty, or property, without due process of law." The Fourteenth Amendment extended this requirement to state governments. There is probably no clause in the Constitution which has produced more litigation than the due process clause. See CONSTITUTIONAL LAW.

duly qualified. Before assuming an office, a person must meet certain legal qualifications. While he may not necessarily possess every qualification for the office, meeting the minimum legal qualifications makes him duly QUALIFIED.

duress. 1. Any wrongful *act* that compels another person to act against his free will. **2.** Any wrongful *threat* through fear of harm that impels a person to act contrary to his natural free will.

dying declaration. A statement made by a person who is aware of his approaching death. Such declarations have special significance in the law of EVIDENCE when they relate to the cause of the injuries from which a person is dying or refer to the person who inflicted these injuries.

E

earnest money. A payment made to bind a bargain or a part payment on a purchase price. Also known as a *deposit* or *down payment*. Compare BINDER.

easement. A specific right which one landowner has over the land of another. The property that enjoys the easement is called the *dominant estate*. The property on which the easement is imposed is called the *servient estate*.

Easements may be created by express language in a written instrument, or they may be created by enjoyment over a period of time with the knowledge and consent of the owner of the servient estate. Such use over a period of years must be open, notorious, and adverse, and must continue over the same period of years as is necessary time for the acquisition of land by ADVERSE POSSESSION. See PRESCRIPTION.

Example 1: John Jones bought a right to draw water from a spring located on the property of his neighbor, Bob Smith. Jones' right to draw water from the spring is an easement.

Example 2: John Smith buys from his neighbor Robert Doe the RIGHT OF WAY and right of INGRESS, EGRESS, AND REGRESS over Doe's lands to reach a public highway. Such right of way and right of ingress, egress, and regress is an easement.

edict. An order or decree promulgated by a sovereign state or by a high official authority.

educational law. There are many branches of educational law. One area is that dealing with the right of freedom of speech for both students and teachers. School administrations such as boards of education and school principals used to be able to control the speech and conduct of students and teachers. Now courts have restricted this authority. Another right recently won by students is the right to use school facilities to hear speakers whom they have invited to address them (this might be called "the right to hear"). Teachers also have freedoms both inside and outside the classroom, and may engage in any political activity they desire to, as long as that activity is not subversive.

One of the fundamental rights of students in public and private educational institutions is the right to DUE PROCESS OF LAW. Dismissal of a teacher or student may come about only after notice, and in some cases a hearing. Teachers and students have the right to counsel and have the right to cross-examine witnesses.

One subject that has been in and out of the courts a great deal is the right of private and parochial schools to receive publicly funded aid. There have been many court decisions involving what forms of government assistance to parochial schools are permissible under the separation of church and state clauses of the Constitution, but the subject has not been settled. In 1947 the United States Supreme Court upheld a New Jersey law authorizing school districts to use public funds to reimburse parents for bus fares of children attending parochial as well as public schools. However, in 1973 the Court declared unconstitutional New York and Pennsylvania laws establishing programs for direct aid and tax credits to parochial schools.

egress. See INGRESS, EGRESS, AND REGRESS.

ejectment. A lawsuit to recover possession of REAL ESTATE. It is a cumbersome process, and in some places where the courts are crowded, an action for ejectment may take years to conclude.

To avoid this lengthy procedure, states have created a remedy for real estate problems arising out of leases. When a landlord wishes to eject a tenant from leased premises, either for nonpayment of rent or for a breach of the lease, the landlord may institute quick legal proceedings to recover possession of the leased premises. These proceedings are known as DISPOSSESS proceedings or SUMMARY proceedings. The law still leaves an action for ejectment intact where there is a dispute as to ownership of land.

ejusdem generis. A phrase (Latin, "of the same kind") used when specific items in law are enumerated and some general language follows that refers to the same kind or class as the specific items previously mentioned.

election. The casting of ballots, counting them, and announcing the results.

In the over-200-year history of the United States, many rules and much law have been established as to how an election should be conducted.

The right to vote is a basic constitutional right. The Fifteenth Amendment to the United States Constitution, ratified in 1870, provides that "The right of citizens of the United States to vote shall not be denied or abridged . . . on account of race, color, or previous condition of servitude."

At COMMON LAW women were ineligible to vote, but the Nineteenth Amendment of the Constitution, ratified in 1920, gave women the right to vote. We all take women's right to vote for granted now, but it was a long, hard struggle to obtain this right.

Prior to 1965 some states imposed literacy and other tests which restricted the right of Negroes or other minority groups to vote. Then in 1965 Congress passed the Voting Rights Act of 1965, which effectively removed these restrictions. The Act expired in 1981. However Congress may vote to extend or reenact the law.

The lawbooks are filled with instances of crooked and irregular elections. Fortunately, our courts have usually protected the rights of citizens and voters and candidates.

Among the restrictions on elections is the regulation of campaign financing. In the early days of American elections there was no restriction on the amount that could be contributed to or expended by contestants. Now there are restrictions placed on the expenditures of money in many state, congressional, and presidential elections. Not only are all candidates required to report contributions and expenditures, but they must disclose to the public the amount spent, and the source of contributions.

election of remedies. Election of remedies is the choice, among several legal remedies, made by a person aggrieved. If he makes a choice of remedies, he is bound and committed to that choice.

> *Example:* John Smith borrows Susan Doe's tractor and does not return it. Doe has a choice. She can either bring an action in REPLEVIN to recover possession of the tractor, or she can sue in a CONVERSION and charge Smith for having converted the tractor to his own use, in which event she may recover a judgment for $900, the full value of the tractor. Doe elects to sue for the value of the tractor. She cannot later change her mind and sue for the tractor itself in an action for replevin. She has definitely made an election of remedies.

electricity laws. Laws relating to the regulation and control of public utilities; the production and sale of electrical light, heat, and power; government ownership of electrical plants; rates and charges to the consuming public; injuries resulting from the production and use of electricity; etc.

eleemosynary. Charitable; an eleemosynary corporation may mean any institution with a benevolent purpose.

emancipation. The act of setting free, as **1.** a MINOR from the legal control and custody of his parents; **2.** slaves (probably the most famous emancipation was that ordered by President Abraham Lincoln during the Civil War); **3.** women from traditional roles.

embargo. 1. A government's prohibition to ship arms and war materiel, usually during wartime. **2.** An edict by a government prohibiting the departure of ships or goods from its ports.

embezzlement. The fraudulent appropriation of another's property by one who has lawful possession of the property, which may have been entrusted to him. Human nature is unfortunately such that positions of trust often bring temptations. Embezzlement is most frequently charged against servants, clerks, employees, agents, partners, bailees, guardians, trustees, executors, administrators, public officials and employees, and attorneys.

A common example of embezzlement is the case of a bank teller who "dips into the till," promising himself that sometime he will replace the stolen money.

embracery. An attempt to corruptly influence a juror, arbiter, referee, or other judicial officer with respect to a verdict, award, or other judicial decision.

emergency. A sudden occurrence that leaves no time for deliberation, though it may require speedy action. Generally in law a person involved with an emergency is not chargeable with failure to use ordinary CARE unless he created the emergency.

eminent domain. The right to take private property for public use. Eminent domain is commonly referred to as the power to condemn land, and most people use the term CONDEMNATION instead of eminent domain.

Originally, the right to take private property for public use was limited to the nation or a state. Then that right was extended to apply to any public use. The right of eminent domain is given public corporations such as municipalities; public bodies such as boards of education; certain public utilities such as oil, gas, and electric companies; street railways; and companies operating wharves, piers, and ferries. The test in every case is whether the property condemned will be subject to public use.

When property is to be taken for public use, legal proceedings are started to determine a fair compensation, generally the FAIR MARKET VALUE, to be paid to the property owner. Determining a fair compensation is generally part of what is called a condemnation proceeding.

Sometimes property is not actually taken for public use but will be injured or damaged by a public project, such as a highway. In such cases the owner is entitled to be paid an amount equal to the damage done to the property.

If only a part of the property is taken, the owner is entitled to be paid the value of the part taken plus any damage to the remainder of the property.

Condemnation proceedings are expensive. Therefore, wherever possible the agency seeking to acquire the property or EASEMENT will purchase the property or easement rather than institute condemnation proceedings.

Example: My father was called a "RIGHT OF WAY man" for a system of electrical railways that operated in upper New York State. The system decided to build an electrical railroad called the Rochester, Syracuse, and Eastern Railroad (R.S.&E.). The company wanted to purchase rights of way for the electrical railroad to operate over the 80 miles between Syracuse and Rochester without the necessity of resorting to the expense of court proceedings to condemn the land. My father was successful in purchasing rights of way from property owners for almost the entire 80 miles; only one property owner in that territory required the company to go to court to condemn the land.

emolument. The incidental profit stemming from an office, public or private—sometimes called a perquisite ("perk") or "lulu."

Example: State legislators spend much money in traveling to and from their places of residence and in staying at the state capital while the legislature is in session. In order to reimburse them for that expense, the legislature passed a bill granting each legislator a lump sum of $4000 per year to cover expenses in traveling to and from the state capital and for living expenses at the state capital. The $4000 was an emolument or perquisite given by the state legislature regardless of whether an individual legislator's expenses equaled, exceeded, or were less than the sum of $4000.

empanel. To prepare a list of persons to serve as jurors. When the list is completed by a clerk or sheriff, it is called a panel of jurors.

encroachment. The act of intruding on another person's property or rights. Somehow most authorities say that an encroachment is a gradual process, but that is not necessarily so. Taking possession of land or airspace which does not belong to one is sufficient to constitute an encroachment. Sometimes placing a fixture over a public street or the land of another person is called an encroachment.

Example: An awning or sign, a part of a roof, or a cornice or water spout may hang over adjoining property and may constitute an encroachment.

encumbrance. Any claim or interest in land held by some person other than the owner.

Example: John Jones buys a farm from Sam Smith for $20,000. He gives Smith $5,000 in cash and executes a MORTGAGE to Smith for $15,000. The mortgage is an encumbrance.

Example: Bob Brown decides to have his house remodeled and re-paired by Joe Black. Brown fails to pay Black for doing the work. Black's bill is $2,500 and Black files a MECHANIC'S LIEN against the house. The mechanic's lien is an encumbrance.

endorse. See INDORSE.

enjoin. To issue an INJUNCTION.

entail. To limit the succession of real estate.

entirety. The whole of something rather than a part of it. In REAL ESTATE law, ownership by a husband and wife by the entirety means that they do not each own a half of the property but each owns the whole proper-ty. An ownership by the entirety means that on the death of the hus-band or wife, the survivor is the owner of the whole (this is called ten-ancy by the entirety). See TENANCY IN COMMON and JOINT TENANCY.

entrapment. In criminal law, the inducement of a potential criminal by police officers or other government agents to commit a crime, so the criminal can be caught red-handed. The claim that an accused person was entrapped may be a defense to a criminal prosecution.

environmental laws. Laws that regulate use of the environment or prohibit its misuse. Environmental law exists at both the federal and the state level. For example, there are many laws on the subject of pollution, including the National Environmental Policy Act of 1969 (N.E.P.A.); the Coastal Zone Management Act (C.Z.M.A.); the Clean Air Act (C.A.A.) and its amendments to reduce the emissions of pollutants into the air. The federal E.P.A. (Environmental Protection Agency) was given the authority to establish national standards of clean air. This agency established the National Ambient Air Quality Standards (N.A.A.Q.S.). Sometimes particular areas had cleaner air than the fed-eral standards required, and then along came new factors which pollut-ed the air and made the air quality deteriorate. The E.P.A. promulgat-ed regulations on the extent of deterioration that would be permitted, called *nondegradation*. Automobile manufacturers under government directions are reducing the pollutants of automobiles.

Many environmental laws are vague and conflicting. As Federal Judge Henry Friendly of the Second Circuit Court of Appeals said, "The N.E.P.A. is so broad yet opaque that it will take even longer than usual fully to comprehend its import."

Federal courts generally have been liberal in granting environmental groups standing in court to prevent or curtail pollution.

equity. 1. A branch of civil law. In order to understand the word in the legal sense, we must look at English history. Equity developed because of the rigidity of the COMMON LAW in certain cases. A LITIGANT who was dissatisfied with the common-law remedy might petition the king for RELIEF. The king in turn referred the matter to his chancellor ("king's conscience"). The chancellor, overburdened with petitions, created a chancellor's court, which became known as the court of CHAN-CERY. This court, later known as the Court of Equity, operated side by side with the common-law courts. Equity as administered by the Court of Equity was based on principles of fairness and justice.

There were now two systems of English courts: a system of law courts and a system of equity courts. These systems were transplanted into the American colonies. Then the American states, with characteristic independence, set up two different systems: Some states combined the branches of law and equity under the administration of the same courts; other states maintained separate courts for law and equity.

It is a basic rule that before a litigant can get relief from the equity branch of court, he must show that he has no adequate remedy on the law side of the court. That is, he cannot get relief or benefits from such conventional lawsuits as a suit to recover some sum of money, a suit for damages for personal injury, a suit for the recovery of personal property, or a suit to eject someone from real estate. Some special circumstances, such as mistakes of fact, FRAUD, or DURESS, require a court of equity to step into the picture. The story of equity relief is a long and complicated one, but essentially it represents an attempt of English and American courts to see that fairness and justice are done.

Over hundreds of years English and American courts have developed statements of principles that have become known as *equity maxims*. Here are some equity maxims, some of which are self-explanatory; the more difficult ones are explicated:

Equity tries to do justice, and not by halves. This means that a court of equity wants to finish the job of justice at one time and not leave anything for future litigation.

Equity favors restitution and seeks to avoid unjust enrichment.

A person who seeks equity must have CLEAN HANDS. This is one of the cardinal rules of equity. It means that equity will not grant relief to anyone who has been overreaching, or who is guilty of fraud or improper conduct.

Equity acts specifically. This principle is difficult to understand. It implies that in law, as distinct from equity, a person may receive damages rather than the thing to which he is entitled; but this is mostly theory because law courts generally give adequate relief.

Equity regards as done that which should have been done. Equity regards a necessary act as having been accomplished.

Where the equities are equal, the law will prevail. That means that where both parties to a controversy stand equally before the court, the court will apply the common-law rules rather than the rules of equity.

Equity does not make the law but assists the law.

Equity does not permit a person to get double satisfaction for the same grievance.

Equity delights in amicable settlements.

2. In real estate jargon, the value of an owner's interest in a property in excess of a mortgage or other encumbrance.

error. A mistake of fact or law in a trial. When there are errors either of fact or of law, the losing party has good grounds for an appeal.

An error of fact generally is based on a misconception of what the true facts are.

Example: A and B had an auto accident. The traffic lights were green for A and red for B. On the trial of the resulting court case, a jury found the traffic lights were red for A. That was an error of fact.

An error of law is an erroneous conclusion drawn from the facts.

Example: A and B had a traffic accident at a street intersection. The traffic light was red for B. The judge charged the jury that B had the right of way. That was a blatant error of law and constituted a RE-VERSIBLE ERROR.

escalator clause. A clause in a contract that provides that when certain factors outside of the contract increase in value, certain benefits within the contract change correspondingly.

Example: A 50-year lease of a building made between John Doe and Henry Smith requires the tenant to pay the landlord the sum of $500 a month. The lease contains an escalator clause that every 5 years during the term of the lease, if the cost of living increases as measured by the Cost of Living Index prepared by the U.S. Department of Labor, the tenant shall pay the landlord a proportionate increase in the rent. At the end of the first 5 years of the lease, the cost of living has increased 50% according to the Cost of Living Index. In accordance with the escalator clause, the tenant is then required to pay a rent increase of 50%, for a total of $750 a month.

escape. The unauthorized leaving of PRISON. Such an escape is of course a serious crime. Almost equally serious is aiding a prisoner to escape. Aid for an escape may come from a fellow prisoner or from someone outside the prison or, more rarely, from a prison officer. In most states, harboring or concealing an escaped prisoner is also a crime.

escheat. Transfer to the state of a person's property when he dies without heirs.

escrow. The delivery of a document or thing to a third party (known as the escrowee), to be delivered by this party to a beneficiary upon the happening of a certain event.

Example: John Jones executes a deed in favor of Richard Roe conveying Blackacre, with the understanding that the deed is to be held in escrow until Mary Jones, sister of John, is paid $3000 by Roe. The deed is delivered in escrow to the Excelsior Bank until it receives proof that Roe has paid $3000 to Mary Jones. The bank is then to deliver the deed to Richard Roe.

esquire. A title given to male persons of high rank or to male owners of large estates. In many parts of the United States, the word, or its abbreviation Esq., is used to refer to a lawyer or member of the bar.

estate. An interest in property. Various kinds of legal estates include the following: (a) an estate in "fee simple," meaning absolute ownership; (b) estates of inheritance; (c) life estates (those held during a person's lifetime); (d) REMAINDER estates (divided into VESTED and CONTINGENT); (e) reversionary estates (property that comes back to the original owner or his heirs); (f) TENANCY IN COMMON (ownership of property by two or more people, each of whom owns an undivided interest in the property); (g) JOINT TENANCY (ownership of property by two or more people with the provision that on the death of one, the property passes to the others); (h) estates of deceased persons.

estate planning. Providing for the disposition of a person's property after his death. Estate planning may be very difficult, because there is often such a time lapse between the execution of a will and the testator's death that during the period family facts and estate facts change considerably. Lawyers and trust officers of banks are those primarily engaged in estate planning to save money for the estate.

estoppel. A doctrine whereby a person who has acted or done something is precluded from taking an inconsistent position to the injury of another. The verb is estop.

> *Example:* Fred Jones had an interest in an abandoned copper mine. Sam Smith made a claim to the mine and for 5 years spent $50,000 a year in restoring the mine. Jones said the mine was no good and had been abandoned by the owners. When the mine yielded copper and prospered because of Smith's money and efforts, Jones was estopped from asserting a claim to the mine.

ethics. See ATTORNEY.

eviction. See DISPOSSESS and EJECTMENT.

evidence. That which is submitted as proof of a fact. Evidence in law usually refers to court testimony and EXHIBITS. There are various kinds of legal evidence, including direct evidence, CIRCUMSTANTIAL EVIDENCE, original evidence, SECONDARY EVIDENCE, positive evidence, negative evidence, probative evidence, etc. Evidence is generally presented by individuals orally in court. The requirement is that in order to be received by a court, evidence must be relevant to the court case. See ADMISSIBLE EVIDENCE.

There is probably no more technical branch of the law than the law of evidence. When evidence is technically unacceptable, it is subject to objection by the adverse party. Objections to evidence may include (a) that it is hearsay, meaning that it consists of statements made by someone other than the witness and is thus not subject to CROSS-EXAMINATION; (b) that it is irrelevant (has no bearing on the matter at hand); (c) that it is IMMATERIAL (does not legally concern the matters in issue); (d) that it is incompetent (wrongfully, illegally, fraudulently, or unconstitutionally obtained or generally inadmissible); (e) that it constitutes the opinion of a nonexpert; (f) that it relates to RES INTER ALIOS ACTA (transactions between persons not parties to the litigation); (g) that it violates the PAROL EVIDENCE RULE; that is, seeks to vary the terms of a written instrument.

There are many exceptions to the hearsay rule. In fact, some people say that the exceptions are so numerous that the hearsay rule is almost a dead letter.

The law of evidence includes *privilege rules,* which means that certain facts should not be disclosed because of confidential relationships. Privileges are based on the theory that benefits result from maintaining confidences in certain relationships. Among the "privileged" relationships are those between husband and wife, attorney and client, doctor and patient, priest and penitent. (There is a dispute as to whether certain facts arising out of the relationship between police and informer, or accountant and client, etc., should be privileged.) Then there are also certain government privileges. Military or state secrets may be privileged if the disclosure of certain information would be harmful to the national interests, military affairs, or international relationships.

Congress has enacted special rules for federal courts. These rules are known as Federal Rules of Evidence. Federal courts throughout the land are gradually interpreting these rules so that someday there may be a separate body of law relating to the Federal Rules of Evidence.

Sometimes it is legally unnecessary in a proceeding to introduce evidence, because the court will take JUDICIAL NOTICE of the facts sought to be proved.

See also PREPONDERANCE, NOTICE TO ADMIT, HYPOTHETICAL, and OPINION EVIDENCE.

ex contractu. A Latin phrase meaning that the transaction in question arises out of a contract.

ex delicto. A Latin phrase meaning "arising out of a wrong": e.g., a TORT, fault, or crime. An action *ex delicto* generally is a tort action.

ex officio. A Latin phrase meaning by virtue of an office or officially; for example, the President of a board generally is a member of all committees of an organization *ex officio,* meaning as part of the duties of his office. The expression also refers to an act done in an official capacity.

> *Example:* The Mayor of New York City greets the Queen of Belgium *ex officio*. That means that the Mayor greets the Queen in his official capacity as Mayor of New York.

ex parte. An application made to a court by one PARTY to a litigation without notice to the other party or giving the other party an opportunity to be heard.

ex post facto law. A law passed by a legislature which makes illegal an act done before the passing of the law. *Ex post facto* laws generally are criminal laws: That is, they make an act retroactively criminal, though it is legal at the time it is committed. *Ex post facto* laws are prohibited by the United States Constitution (Article I, Section 9).

exception. An OBJECTION or notice of nonacquiescence to a ruling made by a judicial officer. Years ago, the function of an exception was to let the judicial officer know that a litigant was dissatisfied with the judicial officer's ruling. The word was frequently used in courtrooms. Now in most states it is the law that where the ruling of a judicial officer is obviously adverse to a litigant's position, the litigant, or the litigant's attorney, need not note an exception.

> *Example:* Lawyer Jones stands up in court to object to the testimony of a witness reading what someone said. Jones objects to the testimony as HEARSAY. The judge overrules the objection. Then Jones says, "Exception," meaning that he disagrees with the judge's ruling. In most states it would be unnecessary for Jones to state an exception, because the judge already knows that Jones has objected to the evidence.

excise tax. A tax other than a tax on property or income. A tax on manufactured articles or articles for sale; a tax on licenses to conduct a trade or pursue an occupation.

execution. 1. A WRIT issued to a sheriff, constable, or marshal directing him to carry out a JUDGMENT of a court, generally calling for the collection of money from the judgment debtor. In some states an execution is called *fi. fa.*, an abbreviation for the Latin phrase FIERI FACIAS, "cause to be done."

To collect on an execution, a constable or marshal may seize any personal property belonging to the judgment debtor (except that exempt by law from execution). This includes crops which have matured, CHOSES IN ACTION, shares of corporate stock, leasehold interests, property in trust, estates in which the judgment debtor has an interest, interest of heirs or next of kin in an estate of a deceased person, money of the judgment debtor, and real estate.

An execution sale must be advertised. Generally an execution sale is made at the courthouse in the county where the execution is carried out.

2. Execution may also mean putting a person to death as legal punishment for a crime.

executors and administrators. An executor (female: executrix) is the person assigned by a will to administer the estate of a deceased person. If the deceased person leaves no will, the person who handles the estate is called the administrator (female: administratrix).

Though the duties of an executor and administrator are fundamentally the same, there are several exceptions. The duties are (a) to collect the assets of the estate; (b) to make an inventory and appraisal of the estate; (c) to pay the decedent's debts; (d) to liquidate the assets of the estate; that is, to convert the assets into cash; (e) to distribute the assets to the person or persons entitled thereto; and (f) to account for what he has received and paid out.

One difference between an executor and an administrator is that generally an executor does not have to file a bond for the faithful performance of his duties, whereas in all cases an administrator does have to file a bond. The other difference is that an executor is required by law to distribute the net assets of the estate to the legatees named in the will and to otherwise carry out the terms of the will. An administrator on the other hand is required to distribute the net assets of the estate to those persons who are entitled to inherit by the laws of the deceased person's residence.

exemplary. In the nature of an example to others. The word is most frequently used in the phrase *exemplary* DAMAGES. Exemplary DAMAGES (sometimes referred to as *punitive damages* or *smart money*) are awarded by juries in cases of severe wrongdoing or malicious, fraudulent, or violent acts on the part of the defendant, and are intended to make up to the plaintiff for mental anguish, shame, or hurt feelings. The law does not permit exemplary damages to be awarded alone; they must be added to other lawful damages.

exemption. 1. Certain property held free from execution by judgment creditors. These laws vary from state to state.

2. A credit allowed under the Internal Revenue Code to reduce the amount of money subject to taxation for children and other dependents who are part of the taxpayer's household, and for persons over 65, blind people, and others.

exhibit. A document or article produced as EVIDENCE at a trial or hearing. Exhibits are kept in order alphabetically (A, B, C, etc.) or numerically (1, 2, 3, etc.). Exhibits become part of the record in the legal proceeding, and have the same weight as other evidence.

expert witness. See HYPOTHETICAL and OPINION EVIDENCE.

express contract. A contract in which the terms are specifically stated by the parties. Compare IMPLIED CONTRACT.

express trust. A TRUST created by a written agreement.

extenuating circumstances. See MITIGATING CIRCUMSTANCES.

extortion. The taking of property or money away from another person by some trick or illegal action. Generally in order to be prosecuted for crime, the extortioner must threaten or otherwise use pressure of office or official right. If money is involved, the amount extorted is usually demanded as a fee for some official duty.

extradition. The surrender by one state or nation to another of a person accused of a crime.

> *Example:* Joe Doakes is indicted for murder in New York State. After the alleged crime, he flees to the State of Iowa, where he is arrested by the Iowa authorities as a fugitive from justice. The governor of New York asks the governor of Iowa to surrender Doakes to stand trial for murder in New York State. The governor of Iowa grants the request. That constitutes an extradition.

eyewitness. A person who can testify as to what he has seen.

F
___

factor. A type of AGENT who bears a FIDUCIARY relationship to his principal and normally cannot delegate any of his authority to a third person without his principal's consent. A factor, sometimes called a *commission merchant,* has implied authority to sell merchandise consigned to him either in his own name or the name of his principal. Among his other powers are those to sell the merchandise for cash or on credit; to collect the purchase price; to extend the time of payment; to insure merchandise entrusted to him; to give the usual warranty on the merchandise.

A factor owes a duty to his principal to obey instructions. He must keep his principal informed of all facts relating to the merchandise; he must account for all money; and of course, being a fiduciary, he must be loyal and aboveboard with his principal.

failure of consideration. In contract law, a lack of the CONSIDERATION or performance required for a valid contract.

failure to look. A principle of law that finds failure to see what is clearly visible INCREDIBLE as a matter of law.

> *Example:* John Smith was about to drive his automobile across a railroad crossing. Smith claims that he looked and didn't see the railroad train bearing down upon the crossing. The court held that his failure to see that which was clearly visible was equivalent to a failure to look, and hence he was not awarded damages for injury.

fair hearing. An impartial hearing before some legal authority. All constitutional safeguards must be given to protect the person charged with wrongdoing. He must be given an opportunity to produce witnesses, and have the assistance of a lawyer, the opportunity to cross-examine adverse witnesses, and the right to make an argument based on the evidence.

fair market value. The just and equitable price an article would bring at a sale under normal conditions; a price at which a willing seller would sell and which a willing buyer would pay provided that each knew all the facts about the property to be sold.

false arrest and imprisonment. Although I treat false ARREST and false IMPRISONMENT together, they are not the same, only first cousins. False arrest may merely be unlawful detention. False imprisonment may be unlawful detention, such as putting someone in confinement unlawfully. Unlawfully putting someone in a jail, asylum, orphanage, or other institution may be false imprisonment. Malice of motive is no part of the wrongs of false arrest or imprisonment; it is, however, an important part of the related wrong or MALICIOUS PROSECUTION.

Arrest or jailing without proper cause, a WARRANT, or other legal process is on its face unlawful. It is the duty of an arresting officer to take a prisoner promptly before a magistrate. It is unlawful to use cruelty or unnecessary force in making an arrest or otherwise detaining a person.

Whenever a lawsuit is brought for unlawful arrest or imprisonment, the most important point to prove is unjustifiable detention, such as the fact that the person was arrested or put in jail without a warrant or legal process; or that the person didn't commit a felony in the presence of the policeman who arrested him, and that therefore the arresting officer had no reasonable grounds to believe that a felony had been committed; or that there was an unreasonable delay in bringing the detained person before a magistrate. It is unnecessary to show that the detained person was eventually acquitted, whereas when a person sues for malicious prosecution, a necessary part of the case is proof that the person charged with the crime was acquitted by a court.

false pretense. MISREPRESENTATION of a fact or facts, with the intent to obtain something from another person illegally. In other words, false pretense is cheating.

> *Example:* Joe Swindelle shows a banker a false personal balance sheet showing that Joe is worth over $100,000. Swindelle obtains a loan of $50,000 from the banker. He misrepresented the true facts. He is not worth a red cent. He is guilty of false pretense.

falsus in uno, falsus in omnibus. The principle that a person who willfully testifies falsely on one matter is apt to testify falsely on other matters. A maxim often included in a judge's INSTRUCTION or CHARGE TO A JURY. See CREDIBILITY.

family court. A COURT that specializes in the handling of controversies between husband and wife and in matters concerning minors not adjudicated in a JUVENILE COURT.

family law. The area of law involving members of a family. It may include marital relations problems; marital support; divorce, annulment, and separation; alienation of affection; illegitimacy and neglected children; custody, support, adoption, and education of children; foster care; federal aid to families with dependent children; unemployed fathers; Social Security benefits; family court; child abuse; paternity SUITS; and juvenile delinquency.

Back in the days of common law in England, husband and wife were regarded legally as one person, but recently many laws have been passed that give women equal rights and remove certain legal disabilities of married women. The result is that the common-law idea of the unity of husband and wife has practically faded away.

family purpose doctrine. A law that makes the head of a family liable for DAMAGES resulting from the negligence of a member of a family while driving the family car. The rule exists in the following 16 states: Alaska, Arizona, Colorado, Connecticut, Georgia, Kentucky, Michigan, Nebraska, Nevada, New Jersey, North Carolina, North Dakota, Oregon, Tennessee, Washington, and West Virginia.

fault. In NEGLIGENCE law, a mistake somebody makes through carelessness or willfulness. American negligence law was formerly founded upon the concept of fault, but this situation is changing. We have a new concept of NO-FAULT in automobile cases, divorce law, and other fields.

federal courts. Courts established by Congress under authority of Article III of the United States Constitution.

federal question. A legal question arising from the interpretation of the United States Constitution, laws of Congress, or a treaty to which the United States is a party. Federal courts have jurisdiction over cases involving federal questions.

Examples of laws of Congress whose interpretation would qualify for federal court jurisdiction include internal revenue laws, patent laws, copyright laws, laws regulating interstate commerce, radio and television, securities acts, and some labor relations laws.

Federal Tort Claims Act. A law passed by Congress in 1946 substantially waiving the federal government's claim to sovereign immunity and permitting suits in United States district courts against the federal government for wrongs committed by the government.

fee. 1. Title to land. 2. Compensation or charge. (If a lawyer charges $500 for handling a case in court, $500 is the lawyer's fee.) 3. The amount charged for a privilege or service. (For example, John Jones pays his neighbor $10 a month for letting him draw water from a spring; the payment is a fee.)

fellow. A member of a college or corporation.

Example: A lawyer may be a fellow of the American College of Probate Counsel or a fellow of the American College of Trial Lawyers. A physician may be a fellow of the College of Surgeons.

fellow servant. An employee working with another employee and employed by the same employer. There is a common-law rule known as the *fellow servant rule* that prohibits an employee from recovering DAMAGES against his employer for injuries caused by the NEGLIGENCE of a fellow servant. Since the days of the first WORKMEN'S COMPENSATION laws (in the 1920s), this rule has been done away with, and employees are automatically compensated for their injuries sustained IN THE COURSE OF employment.

felon. A person who is convicted of a FELONY; in other words, a criminal who has committed and has been convicted of a serious crime.

felonious. Having the attributes of a felon or felony; to do something feloniously means to do it criminally or unlawfully.

felony. A serious crime punishable by imprisonment, or in some cases by death.

fence. See RECEIVING STOLEN GOODS.

fiat justitia ruat coelum. A Latin sentence meaning "Let justice be done though the heavens fall" that appears in courthouses and public buildings throughout the country to point to the ideal of the law.

fidelity bond. A BOND indemnifying an employer against loss due to an employee's dishonesty. If the employee defaults or embezzles and the employer loses money, the employer may collect from the insurance company that issued the bond. Cashiers and other employees who frequently handle money are routinely *bonded*.

fiduciary. A person holding a position of trust. The classic example is an EXECUTOR or trustee, but the law extends the obligation of trust to many persons, including an AGENT, an ATTORNEY, a partner, etc.

fieri facias. See EXECUTION.

file. To place with an officer of the court a paper or document, a procedure that may have considerable legal significance.

Example: The federal rules require that an action in federal court be instituted by filing the complaint in the action with a clerk of the United States District Court.

filiation. A legal proceeding to legitimize an illegitimate child. See BASTARD and ILLEGITIMACY.

finding. A decision by a court or a jury.

fine. A sum of money imposed by a court as penalty for a crime or offense.

fine print. See CARRIER and INSURANCE.

fiscal year. See TAXABLE YEAR.

fixed assets. An accounting term meaning assets, such as land, buildings, or machinery, that are used directly in the operation of a business.

fixture. Personal property attached to real property with the intention that it will become a permanent addition to the real property. The law that governs fixtures depends on a number of factors, including the relationship between the owners of the personal property and the real property, the method of attaching the personal property to the building, any agreement or leases involved, the character of the personal property, etc.

> *Example:* John Jones leases a store from Sam Smith. Smith and Jones sign a lease. The lease provides that no property nailed to the leased premises may be removed by Jones at the end of the term of the lease. Jones nails certain shelves and counters to the building. They thereby become fixtures and part of the building.

flagrante delicto. A Latin phrase literally meaning "while the crime is blazing"; one caught FLAGRANTE DELICTO is caught in the act of committing a crime or wrong.

force majeure. A French phrase meaning "major force." Some people use the term to mean ACT OF GOD. It also means an irresistible force.

forcible entry and detainer. 1. Forcibly taking possession of land or keeping possession of it against others. **2.** In most states, a statutory proceeding to regain possession of land by the rightful owners or to protect the owners from unlawful invasion. In other words, it is a proceeding seeking an order of the court ejecting those who have unlawfully entered upon land or preventing those who seek to take unlawful possession of land. This proceeding is a speedy one to give immediate RELIEF to the owner of the land.

foreclosure. A term generally applied to MORTGAGES, a foreclosure cuts off or eliminates the right of redemption. In EQUITY if a person fails to make mortgage payments due, the debtor can regain the property: that is, he can buy it back before the foreclosure has become final. That right to buy the mortgaged property back is called the *equity of redemption.* In a *mortgage foreclosure* suit in court, the purpose is to put a stop to the mortgagor's equity of redemption, so when the property is sold after the mortgagor has defaulted, the sale of the mortgaged property will be final and good for all time.

foreman of the jury. The member of the JURY who presides over it and speaks for it. Generally the judge, on the advice of the district attorney, selects the foreman of a GRAND JURY; on a PETIT JURY, the jurists select their own foreman.

forensic medicine. The application of medical knowledge in legal cases. Some people claim that forensic medicine is the scientific field of medicine used in law cases (in other words, that it is a branch of medicine), but I don't think so. I think that lawyers can make a special study of medicine and become experts in the field of forensic medicine.

foreseeable. Referring to that which should be anticipated. In the law of NEGLIGENCE foreseeability may affect a person's LIABILITY.

> *Example:* John Smith runs a lumber mill. In that lumber mill he uses highly dangerous machinery without adequate safeguards to prevent accidents to his employees. That accidents will happen in Smith's mill is foreseeable.

forfeit. To lose a right to which one would otherwise be entitled; to relinquish.

> *Example:* John Jones pays $100 for an OPTION to buy a certain piece of real estate within 30 days for $20,000. The option provides that if he does not exercise the option within 30 days, he loses the $100. Jones does not exercise the option to buy within the 30 days and therefore forfeits the $100.

forgery. The false making or alteration of a written INSTRUMENT to effect a FRAUD—a serious crime. Many people think of forgery only as imitating another's signature, but that is only one example of forgery.

forthwith. As soon as possible or in the immediate future.

forum. A court of justice or administrative board where a particular controversy is heard. Often the question arises as to whether the court should apply the law of the place of the forum (LEX FORI), or the law of the place where a contract was made (LEX LOCI CONTRACTUS) or a wrong committed (LEX LOCI DELICTUS). See CONFLICT OF LAWS.

forum non conveniens. A Latin phrase meaning "unsuitable forum"; a doctrine that a particular court may refuse to hear a case because the case should be heard in some other jurisdiction either for the convenience of witnesses or in the interests of justice. See CHANGE OF VENUE.

franchise. A privilege conferred by the government, a person, or a corporation on an individual or company, such as (a) the right to use public property for a specific purpose, (b) the privilege given by Sheraton Corporation of America to use the name Sheraton in connection with a hotel.

franchise tax. A tax that a corporation has to pay for a privilege granted by a government.

fraud. A wrong committed to cheat or deceive another person. In order for the act to be fraudulent, it must be a breach of a legal duty. Fraud takes on a number of forms and enters into many fields. A common example is when the perpetrator of a fraud makes a false representation of fact, knowing that the representation is false and intending that the falsity of the representation will deceive some person to that person's injury. Subjects of false representation include the financial condition or solvency of some person or company; the location of or boundaries of a parcel of real estate; the worth or value of property or the income of certain property.

fraudulent conveyances. This subject is closely related to the subject of FRAUD but deserves special attention. When a debtor transfers his property and assets beyond the reach of his creditors, that is called a fraudulent CONVEYANCE. In this situation the law favors creditors, so that when a debtor divests himself of property, the law generally allows creditors to pursue the property transferred for the purpose of nullifying creditors' rights. Although we think of fraudulent conveyances as applying largely to real estate, the law of fraudulent conveyances applies to fraudulent transfers of other kinds of property, including tangible personal property, bank accounts, earnings and wages, insurance policies, and patents.

free and clear. Unencumbered by any LIEN or MORTGAGE or any other factor which would make the TITLE to real property unmarketable. See CLEAR TITLE.

freedom of speech and of the press. These rights are guaranteed by the United States Constitution and most state constitutions. See CONSTITUTIONAL LAW.

freehold. An interest in REAL ESTATE.

full. Legally complete and abundant.

full covenant deed. See DEED and COVENANT.

full faith and credit. The United States Constitution, Article IV, Section 1, provides: "Full faith and credit shall be given in each State to the public Acts, Records, and Judicial Proceedings of every other State." This doctrine, known as COMITY OF STATES, means that court orders, judgments, statutes, and records of the various states shall have the same force and effect throughout the United States to which they would be entitled in their own state.

fungible. Belonging to a class, one specimen of which is as good as another and interchangeable with it. For example, certain classes of wheat or rice are fungible; on the other hand, horses, dogs, and other domestic animals are nonfungible because they are individually different and not interchangeable.

future earnings. Anticipated earnings, which may be an element of DAMAGES in personal INJURY suits if the injury adversely affects these potential earnings.

future interest. A phrase generally used in connection with property, meaning that someone may have the privilege of enjoyment or possession in the future but not at the present time.

> *Example:* John Smith gives his daughter, Helen, a life interest in his farm and also provides in his will that on his daughter's death the farm will go to his grandson, Joe. Joe has a future interest in the land.

G

---

garnishment. A legal proceeding whereby a creditor seeks to recover a debtor's money or property held in the hands of a third party. The procedure varies from state to state. The money or property in the hands of the third party may be earnings or wages due the debtor; rent from real estate; a promissory note; proceeds of an insurance policy; dividends from corporate stock; a legacy; or income from an annuity. The proceeding to obtain the debtor's money or property is called a garnishment, and the third party from whom the money or property is sought is called the garnishee. (The proceeding itself is sometimes erroneously referred to in slang as a "garnishee.")

> *Example:* John Doe obtains a judgment against Richard Roe for $500. Roe works as a foreman in the factory of the Excelsior Company for a salary of $500 a week. The law of that state permits a garnishment of up to 10% of wages. Doe obtains a garnishment order vs. the Excelsior Company, requiring them to pay to Doe the sum of $50 a week, subtracted from Roe's salary, until the judgment of $500 is paid in full.

gerrymander. To divide a state, territory, or voting district in order to accomplish a political or improper purpose. For example, the county of X is normally Democratic: that is, it generally elects candidates sponsored by the Democratic Party. Some Republican politicians may figure out a way to divide up the county into districts so that the result is to elect a few Republican legislators instead of all Democratic. (The term is derived from the name of a redistricter, Gerry, who created a district that looked rather like a sala*mander*.)

gift. In law there are two principal kinds of gifts: gifts *inter vivos* (Latin, "between the living") and gifts CAUSA MORTIS (Latin, "in case of death"). A gift *inter vivos* is a gift from one living person to another. It is an absolute gift. In order for a gift *inter vivos* to be valid, there must be (a) a donor and a donee; (b) an intent to make the gift final; (c) property which is the subject of the gift; (d) delivery of the gift, actual or symbolic; (e) acceptance by the donee.

gift taxes. Gift taxes imposed by the federal government have gone through four phases: (a) During the nineteenth century and the first quarter of the twentieth century there were no gift taxes. That meant that wealthy individuals, whose estates would be subject to substantial federal or estate taxes, avoided those taxes by giving away substantial sums of money or property to those persons who would be their natural beneficiaries. (b) In 1924 the federal government imposed gift taxes of about three quarters the amount of the taxes assessed against estates. In many cases that still furnished an incentive to make gifts and ultimately save taxes. (c) In 1976 the statute was changed so that the rates of taxes for gift taxes and federal estate taxes became the same so that there was no longer any advantage in paying gift taxes rather than federal estate taxes. Except for relatively small gifts, there was no advantage in making gifts prior to death. (d) In 1981 Congress again changed the federal gift tax law so that, among other things, there is no gift tax on gifts of up to $10,000 per year for each donee. That is, if a wealthy person has twelve grandchildren and wishes to save taxes by making lifetime gifts to the grandchildren, each year he can give each grandchild money or property valued up to the sum of $10,000. That means that $120,000 of gifts per year would not be subject to taxation. Further, an individual can make unlimited gifts to his or her spouse without incurring gift tax.

good and marketable title. A CLEAR TITLE to real estate, free from any reasonable suspicion that there is anything wrong with it. Compare UNMARKETABLE TITLE.

good and workmanlike manner. In law a worker is worthy of his hire and should be paid, provided he performs his work in a good and workmanlike manner. That means that he must do the work with the same degree of skill that other workers in his community and occupation use.

good behavior. Proper behavior as a condition for something. The phrase is often used when a person found guilty of a crime is put on PROBATION. That is, the judge may place the defendant on probation for as long as the defendant lives as a peaceful and law-abiding citizen. A prisoner may have his time to be served reduced for good behavior. Some officials, including federal judges, hold their offices for life or during good behavior.

good cause. A valid reason for legal action. In other words, if good cause is shown, a court may take a certain action.

good consideration. A loose phrase sometimes used as the equivalent of VALUABLE CONSIDERATION. Good consideration may be money or property, or it may even sometimes be so-called "love and affection."

good faith. Observance of honest intent. A person who acts honestly and is free from knowledge or suspicion of any wrongdoing in connection with a transaction acts in good faith. (Of course, this is the opposite of bad faith.)

goods, wares, and merchandise. This phrase is a good example of legal verbosity; it really means personal property. Then why not say so? Because lawyers are victims of tradition and habit.

> *Example:* The Smith Company, a wholesale hardware dealer, sells hammers, screwdrivers, and wrenches to the Jones Company, a retailer. The Jones Company does not pay the bill on time, so the Smith Company sues the Jones Company for the price of the tools. In the suit papers, the lawyer for the Smith Company says the Smith Company sold to the Jones Company "goods, wares, and merchandise," consisting of hammers, screwdrivers, wrenches, and other tools of an agreed value of $3,000, to be paid in 30 days. Why didn't the lawyer say "tools" instead of "goods, wares, and merchandise?" The answer is because the lawyer, his father, and his grandfather had been using that phrase since time immemorial.

gore. In real estate law, a small irregular piece of land, often triangular in shape, that doesn't go with the land surrounding it that is being conveyed.

government. The political agency that administers, exercises the powers of, and carries out the purposes of a nation, state, city, county, or other political subdivision.

grand jury. A jury that considers an accusation of crime and decides whether or not to return an INDICTMENT. See TRUE BILL. The grand jury is an ancient institution, going back to common-law days in England. Its primary purpose is to inquire into crimes committed within its jurisdiction (generally a county). It functions as a charging body and does not itself determine guilt or innocence. The grand jury is peculiarly a democratic institution in that it may prevent persons from being charged with crimes on insufficient EVIDENCE, and it acts to bring to justice persons accused of crime where there is evidence to support the accusation.

grand larceny. See LARCENY.

grant. 1. To transfer, to confer, or to bestow some particular right or property to a person. The term applies mostly to real estate and is used in deeds or real estate contracts to mean "to transfer and convey." **2.** To allow or give: for example, a judge or a court grants an order, decree, injunction, or decision. A government or philanthropic organization grants money to worthy causes and projects.

grantee, grantor. A grantee is a person to whom real estate is conveyed by deed. A grantor is the person owning the real estate, who executes a deed of the property to someone else.

gravamen. The essential part of a court case.

> *Example:* Jane Smith sues Mary Brown for breaking her contract of employment and files a complaint. The gravamen of this cause of action is BREACH OF CONTRACT.

grievance. 1. A claim that one's legal rights have been violated. **2.** In labor law, a procedure to determine whether a party to a collective bargaining agreement has violated the agreement.

ground rent. 1. When a conveyance of land is made and the grantor reserves rent to himself in perpetuity or for a long period of time (say, 99 years), the rent reserved to be paid to the grantor is called ground rent. **2.** Rent paid for the right to occupy and improve the land, e.g. by putting a building on it.

group insurance. Insurance provided by a contract between an insurance company and the employees of a particular company or members of another group to cover the members of that group.

grouping of contacts. See CONFLICT OF LAWS.

guaranty. 1. A promise to stand back of and, if necessary, pay the debt of another. **2.** An undertaking to perform a contract which someone else has primarily agreed to perform (see STATUTE OF FRAUDS). In other words, the contract or guaranty may be a promise that if necessary, one will pay another's debt or perform another's contract. The one making the guaranty is called the guarantor and the person to whom the promise is made is called the guarantee. (Sometimes a guaranty is misspelled or loosely called a guarantee.) Generally guaranty contracts must be in writing.

guardian. A person or institution the law assigns to care for the person or property of a MINOR or, in some states, an INCOMPETENT person. (In many states people who look after the person or property of incompetent people other than minors are called COMMITTEES.) The person for whom a guardian is appointed is called a WARD.

A guardianship of the person or property is a position of utmost trust.

There are three kinds of guardians: (a) guardian of the person, (b) guardian of the property, and (c) guardian of the person and property. A guardian of the person is charged with supervising the support, education, and religious training of the ward. A guardian of the property is charged with the responsibility of handling the ward's property, making proper investments, collecting the income, and making expenditures on the ward's behalf. Aside from natural guardians (parents), guardians are appointed by a court or a will. Ordinarily, no guardian of the person or property may be appointed when one or more of a child's parents are living, because the parents as natural guardians have full responsibility for the upbringing of the child and the handling of the child's property.

A guardian is usually required to give a BOND conditional on the satisfactory performance of his duties. However, banks or trust companies appointed as guardians are not required to file bonds.

guardian *ad litem*. A guardian appointed by a court to prosecute or defend a CIVIL ACTION in behalf of a MINOR.

guest. This word has legal significance when a guest is injured on someone's property. The guest may be a social or a business guest (sometimes called in law an *invitee*) or a *licensee.* The obligation of the property owner may differ toward different categories.

The characterization of a licensee (someone who has been given permission to enter property for a specific purpose) may seem technical, but the distinction between LIABILITY to a licensee or invitee and to a trespasser ordinarily is that to licensees or invitees the landlord owes only the duty of active care, whereas to a trespasser the landlord owes only the duty of not intentionally inflicting injury on him except for self-protection. A landlord must take responsibility to inform either the guest, licensee, or trespasser of a dangerous condition on the premises. There are some courts that say that a property owner owes a higher degree of care for the protection of a social guest than a business guest, on the theory that he expects a profit or economic benefit from a business guest. All in all, the subject is highly technical and is subject to changing rules. In fact, there is a trend on the part of some courts to depart from the old interpretation of guest, licensee, or trespasser. Those courts simply ask, "Did the owner of property know of a dangerous condition or warn the licensee, guest, or trespasser?"

Some states have *guest statutes,* which provide that the owner of an automobile is not liable to his guests for any injuries that they receive in an accident unless those injuries were caused by the wanton or willful acts (e.g., drunkenness) of the car owner. Some people regard guest statutes as harsh, since in many cases they prevent guest passengers from recovering for their injuries. On the other hand, the advocates of guest statutes claim that those statutes prevent collusion between car owners and their passengers, often friends or relatives, to frame cases against insurance companies.

guilty. Referring to a person convicted of a crime or a person who confesses a crime. A jury uses this term when it convicts a person accused of crime. A person may of course *be* guilty of a crime even though he is not arrested or tried in court. However, according to the DUE PROCESS OF LAW clauses of the Constitution, he is *legally* innocent until proved guilty and convicted.

H

---

habeas corpus. A Latin phrase, referring to an ancient WRIT that means "you have the body." It has been called the most famous writ in English law. As a practical matter today it is a court order directing someone (generally a sheriff or jailor) to produce a detained person in order for the court to determine if that person is being unlawfully detained. The ancient writ was carried over into this country by the English colonists, and after the American Revolution it was incorporated into the state constitutions. The United States Constitution (Article I, Section 9) provides that *habeas corpus* shall not be suspended unless public safety requires it in the case of rebellion or invasion.

Under a writ of *habeas corpus,* a judge must scrutinize the facts carefully to see if a person is unlawfully deprived of liberty. An immediate hearing is required, and if the person is found to be unlawfully detained, he must be released immediately. There is no fooling around when a writ of *habeas corpus* is issued. It is a fundamental American right—a safeguard of personal liberty. Our lawbooks are full of court cases in which *habeas corpus* has in fact preserved personal liberty.

Example: A state legislature gave cities the local option of prohibiting the establishment of gambling casinos. The city of Hamilton didn't exercise the local option to prohibit gambling casinos. John Doe operated a gambling casino in Hamilton. Local officials interpreted the state law as prohibiting the operation of gambling casinos throughout the state. They arrested Doe and had him put in jail. Doe had his lawyer go to the local judge, who issued a writ of *habeas corpus* directed to the city jailor to bring Doe before him immediately. The judge held that Doe was illegally detained and ordered him released at once.

habendum. A clause in most deeds that refers to ownership. American and English lawyers call the words "to have and to hold" in a deed the *habendum* clause, though the complete Latin phrase for the words "to have and to hold" is *habendum et tenendum*.

habitable. When used in the law, a term meaning "tenantable." Premises are habitable or tenantable when they are fit for human occupancy. See UNTENANTABLE.

Example: A neighborhood was infested with rats. The rats seemed to make their headquarters at one property owned by landlord Jones. Jones' tenants refused to pay rent until he took steps to free the building of rats. The premises were not habitable as long as the rats were there. The judge agreed with the tenants and required Jones to hire an exterminator to get rid of the rats.

half-truth. A statement that is literally true but that creates a false impression.

Example: The XYZ Company made a lot of money for 3 years in a row; then its earnings declined for the next 7 years. The company put out a public statement that its average earnings for the past 10 years showed a profit. That was literally true, in that if you took the total earnings of the past 10 years and divided by 10, the average earnings showed a profit. The misleading part of the statement was that the company for the last 7 years showed a substantial loss and the company now is in poor financial condition.

harmless error. A mistake of law which an appellate or reviewing court considers not of sufficient consequence to have affected the result in the lower court, and not of sufficient consequence to warrant a reversal of the decision of the lower court.

hear ye. See OYEZ.

hearing. A session of a court or an arm of the court. Rights at a hearing include the right to be heard, to cross-examine witnesses, and to present evidence. According to the United States Constitution, any hearing must be fair and impartial. Notice of the time and place of the hearing must be given to all parties affected by it. A party affected by the hearing may appear in person or be represented by his attorney.

hearsay evidence. See EVIDENCE.

heir. In a technical sense, a person who stands to inherit property when there is no will. Colloquially, the word is used to designate any person who inherits property.

heir apparent. One who has the right of inheritance provided he lives longer than the person from whom he would inherit.

heir presumptive. A person who, if a relative dies, would under present circumstances be the heir of that relative. But it is understood that that right of inheritance may be defeated by some event, such as the birth of a closer relative. A king's eldest daughter is his heir presumptive unless and until the king has a son, in monarchies based on male succession.

henceforth. In the future, or from now on. Often used in statutes or legal documents.

hereafter. At some future date, or subsequently. Another word frequently used in statutes and legal documents.

hereby. Done now by this means. Another word frequently used by lawyers.

hereditament. Anything that can be inherited, whether personal property or real estate.

heretofore. Formerly; in the past.

hereunder. Authorized by this statute or legal document.

herewith. A legalese term meaning some document accompanies the letter of transmittal in which the word is used.

highway. A road open to the public. A highway may be established by continued public use over a long period of time. The legislature of a state may establish the course of a highway, or it may delegate authority to do so to a highway department or a board of public works. The state (or the county, the town, or other appropriate political subdivision) has the right to control and the obligation to maintain highways.

holder in due course. One who has taken a NEGOTIABLE instrument with the understanding that he has no knowledge of anything that would impair the validity of that instrument; he has acquired the negotiable instrument for value and in good faith.

holding company. A corporation that owns or has a controlling interest in one or more other corporations. Sometimes referred to as *controlling company.*

holograph. A document wholly handwritten by the person who signs it. A *holographic will* is a will entirely written, dated, and signed by the testator. It is valid without proof or other formalities in a number of states.

homestead laws. 1. Homestead laws were enacted in the United States to protect families against claims of creditors. The laws created exemptions so that the homestead (family residence) could not be sold to satisfy the owners' debts. In some states owners of homesteads are given a limited tax exemption. **2.** During pioneer days, under homestead laws of that time, migrating settlers could claim public lands as their own by living and working on specified numbers of acres—often 160, ¼ square mile—for a certain number of years.

homicide. I used to think that the word "homicide" meant a murder. I was wrong. Homicide is a much broader term than murder. It means any killing of a human being, intentional or unintentional. MURDER is the intentional killing of a human being—and here is the important part of the definition of murder—*with* MALICE. MANSLAUGHTER, which may be intentional or unintentional, is the unpremeditated killing of a human *without malice.*

hostile witness. An unfriendly witness or one whose relationship to the opposing party to the lawsuit creates a presumption that his testimony will be favorable to the opposing party. A hostile witness may be asked LEADING QUESTIONS by the party calling him.

humanitarian doctrine. See LAST CLEAR CHANCE.

hung jury. A jury that cannot unanimously agree on a verdict, or in some cases cannot arrive at a 10-to-2 verdict.

husband and wife. See FAMILY LAW.

hush money. Money paid someone to keep silence; often it is a bribe.

hypothecate. To pledge something as security for a loan. Hypothecating usually does not require the promisor or the person to whom the loan is made to deliver the property which is hypothecated.

hypothetical. Referring to something assumed factual for present purposes, though not necessarily true. *Hypothetical statement,* or *hypothesis,* enters into many fields of law. The use of *hypothetical questions* in the examination of expert witnesses used to be very popular. Experts, who (unlike other witnesses) are permitted by law to give OPINION EVIDENCE would be asked to assume a set of facts and then would be asked something like this: "Assume, doctor, the facts I have just given you. Can you form and express an opinion as to whether the injuries which I have just described to you are or are not permanent?" The doctor's correct answer would be that he could form and state such an opinion. Then he would be asked to give his opinion.

Today hypothetical questions are not so favored by law as formerly. In most cases the expert is simply asked to give an opinion without being asked the hypothetical question.

I

ibidem (**ibid., ib.**) Latin, "in the same place." In a CITATION, it means something is to be found in the same place as the preceding reference.

id est (**i.e.**). Latin, meaning "that is," or "that is to say." (Not necessarily a legal phrase, but commonly used in legal writing.)

idem (**id.**). A Latin word meaning "same," often used by writers to refer to the same authority.

> *Example:* An author quotes a famous court decision as an authority for a legal proposition. He then cites another statement of law, after which he writes in parentheses *"idem,"* meaning the authority is the same.

identification. Proof in court that a person or thing is the same as the person or thing referred to. Although the question of identification occasionally becomes the issue in a civil case, it more frequently arises in a criminal case.

> *Example:* Johnny Upstart is arrested for purse snatching. He or his photograph is brought before the victim for identification. The victim says that Upstart is the same person who stole her purse. Or Upstart may be placed in a *police lineup* to determine if he is the person involved in the purse snatching.

idiot. A person born mentally defective or who has suffered an accident or disease that causes extreme mental defectiveness.

ignorantia legis neminem excusat. A Latin phrase which has become a maxim of law: "Ignorance of the law excuses no one."

illegal. Contrary to law; something that is illegal is wrong or unlawful.

illegitimacy. A status that is counter to law; the word is used particularly to refer to the status of a BASTARD. See PATERNITY SUIT and LEGITIMATION.

illicit. Prohibited or unlawful. The word is used particularly to refer to unlawful sexual relationships, and to narcotics.

immaterial. In the law of EVIDENCE, having no legal relationship to the subject at issue.

> *Example:* John Smith is charged with reckless driving on New Year's Day. The opposing lawyer offers to prove that Smith was convicted of drunken driving on the preceding Christmas Day. Smith's lawyer objects because the proposed evidence is immaterial and related to another instance, time, and place. The judge sustains Smith's lawyer's objection and refuses to allow the proposed evidence.

immigration. An alien's entering a country for the purpose of establishing a residence. In the United States, immigration is governed by quotas and many other restrictions. Immigration laws are administered by the Immigration and Naturalization Service in Washington.

immunity. Freedom from some duty or legal obligation. It may mean an exemption from performing some duty which other citizens have to perform; it may refer to an exemption from taxation; or it may refer to a privilege granted to certain citizens.

A privilege formerly frequently used is governmental immunity. It was derived from an old English doctrine that you could not sue the government because, old English law said, "The King can do no wrong." The doctrine has been abandoned by most states. See FEDERAL TORT CLAIMS ACT.

impartiality. Freedom from interest in a matter in controversy, or freedom from bias, passion, or prejudice.

> *Example:* John Smith was drawn to serve as a member of a panel of jurors to try cases at a term of court. In one of the cases the XYZ Company was named as a defendant. Smith was a stockholder in the XYZ Company. Smith was not allowed to serve as a juror in the case, because he had a pecuniary interest in the XYZ Company and therefore would not be an impartial juror.

impeach. 1. To bring a public officer before a tribunal on a charge of wrongdoing. 2. In the broad meaning, to blame, censure, or disparage a person. 3. The most common legal meaning relates to witnesses in court. Attempts are often made by the opposing side to *impeach a witness,* that is, to discredit his testimony in the eyes of the jury or judge.

impediment. 1. An obstruction or obstacle such as a fence or physical barrier. 2. A personal incapacity or disability. 3. Some intangible thing, such as a contract or a previous marriage, which is a hindrance to a legal status.

implied. Intended or indicated to be so, though not directly or expressly stated. An *implied warranty,* for example, means that a seller of goods warrants that they are fit and suitable for the purpose intended even though he does not give the buyer a written warranty.

implied contract. A contract that may be fairly inferred from surrounding circumstances. This phrase may become very important in law. A contract may be assumed by implication from the conduct of the parties, even though there is no formal offer and acceptance (necessary ingredients of an *expressed contract*).

> *Example:* John Jones owns an apartment house. He hired Sam Smith to work for him as janitor of the apartment house for a period of 3 months at $180 a week. When the 3 months were up, Smith wasn't expressly rehired, but he continued to serve as janitor of the apartment house. At the end of 6 months Smith said he wanted some money. Jones said, "Nothing doing. I hired you for 3 months and that is all. What you did after 3 months made you a mere volunteer." A court held that at the end of 3 months Jones accepted the services of Smith and had made an implied contract to hire him. Therefore Jones was liable to Smith for $180 a week for the additional 3 months.

imply. To make something fairly understood without spelling it out. In law, people's actions or speech may make something clear by inference, even though it is not expressly stated in words or writing. In such a case the actions or speech of people may imply certain legal consequences.

impost. A TAX or duty.

imprisonment. Legally, any detention of a person by force or against his will. If a person is deprived of liberty, or compelled to remain where he doesn't wish to remain or go where he doesn't want to go, that is imprisonment. It is not necessary that the person be sent to jail or prison.

imputed negligence. NEGLIGENCE of one person ascribed to or attributed by law to another. It may exist because of the special relationship between the person who is actually negligent and the person to whom negligence is ascribed where such relationship implies an element of control.

> *Example:* Robert Roe owns a Cadillac automobile, which is driven by his chauffeur, Richard Smith. One morning while driving Roe to work, Smith had an accident, injuring a pedestrian. The pedestrian claimed that Smith ran a red light. Any negligence of Smith is imputed to Roe.

in camera. A Latin phrase meaning "in a room"; in CHAMBERS. Certain legal proceedings or hearings are held *in camera*—in the judge's office, from which the public is excluded.

in esse. A Latin phrase meaning "in being," often used in law to refer to children who are alive when a certain event happens.

in extremis. A Latin phrase sometimes used in law meaning "in a last illness."

in futuro. In the future.

in haec verba. This Latin phrase means "in these words." It is sometimes used in law to mean "in this precise language."

in kind. Of the same kind or quality.

in lieu of. In substitution for or instead of. This phrase is not necessarily a legal phrase, but lawyers use it often.

in loco parentis. A Latin phrase meaning "in place of a parent." A guardian or a court performing a parent's rights and duties may be said to be acting *in loco parentis.*

in omnibus. A Latin phrase meaning "in all things." Sometimes in legal language it is used to mean "in every respect."

in pari delicto. A Latin phrase meaning "in equal fault." In criminal law a person who is *in pari delicto* is equally responsible for the crime with one or more other persons.

in perpetuity. Perpetually; intended to exist forever.

in personam. Referring to legal or equitable actions directed against individual persons. See IN REM.

in re. In the matter of, or concerning a particular thing. This phrase is not necessarily a legal phrase. In fact, it is used commonly in business correspondence. In law it is often used for the title of a legal proceeding.

> **Example:** If a proceeding is instituted to close Jones Street, the proceeding would be entitled "*In re* the application to close Jones Street."

in rem. Referring to a legal or equitable proceeding directed against a particular property. See IN PERSONAM.

in solido. A Latin phrase meaning "as a whole." It is used in wills or trust instruments when a number of trusts are created. The trustee may be authorized to treat the corpus of the trusts *in solido,* meaning that he may treat the aggregate of the various trusts as one entity without breaking it into individual parts.

in the course of. During and directly related to. A phrase used in WORKMEN'S COMPENSATION cases. More fully stated, it is "arising out of and in the course of employment." It means that a person is covered for workmen's compensation benefits if his accident or illness arises out of and in the course of his employment.

inadmissible. Not receivable in EVIDENCE.

Example: John Doe and Richard Roe enter into a written contract whereby Doe agrees to sell Roe three horses at $3000 a horse. Roe claims that as part of the deal they had a verbal agreement that if Roe liked the horses, he could buy five additional horses at $3000 a horse. Evidence of the verbal agreement was inadmissible (see PAROL EVIDENCE RULE) because it varied from the terms of the written agreement.

inalienable. Something not able to be bought, transferred, sold, or distributed.

incest. Sexual relations between close blood relatives who would be legally prohibited from marrying each other.

inchoate. Incomplete or imperfect.

Example of inchoate right of dower: There are two kinds of dower: (a) that in which the wife survives her husband. In such a case the dower is complete and she is usually entitled to a third of the income from her husband's property; (b) that in which the husband is still alive. This kind of dower is inchoate because the right of dower is incomplete; that is, the wife gets no dower while her husband is alive.

income tax. A TAX owing to a state or federal government based on a person's or corporation's net income.

incompatibility. A word used in divorce proceedings, meaning that the parties are unable to live in harmony.

incompetence. Inability or unfitness or lack of qualification to perform certain acts.

incompetent. A person who is incapable of managing one's own affairs. Such incapacity may be due to a mental deficiency, immaturity, or senility. (An incompetent may be subject to UNDUE INFLUENCE.)

Example: John Smith is 90 years of age and has become forgetful and irresponsible. He is incapable of looking after his affairs. His children apply to court for the appointment of the Excelsior Bank as COMMITTEE of John Smith, an incompetent. The bank takes possession of Smith's property, inventorying his property, making investments, and from the net income paying Smith's living expenses and all of his bills.

incontrovertible. About which there can be no dispute.

Example: Lawyer Smith stands up in court and says, "It is incontrovertible that Main Street in this town runs north and south." If this is true, Smith's statement is incontrovertible.

incorporate. To form a CORPORATION.

incorporeal. Intangible; literally, "not of the body."

incredible. Not worthy of belief, and referring to that which no reasonably intelligent person would believe. See FAILURE TO LOOK.

> *Example:* There is an old case in which a high court said, "Not to see that which is plainly visible is incredible as a matter of law."

incriminating circumstance. In criminal law, a fact which would indicate that some person has committed or been involved in the commission of a crime.

incriminating statement. A statement made by a person that indicates his guilt. This differs from a CONFESSION, which is an acknowledgment of guilt, in that an incriminating statement may be made without intending such an acknowledgment.

incumbent. A person presently holding an office or a position.

indemnify. To agree to pay another person for loss, or to protect or to hold another person harmless from INJURY or damage.

Generally an obligation to indemnify arises out of an express contract, but it may also arise out of an IMPLIED CONTRACT. When a person has to pay a sum of money that another should have paid, the person who should have paid the money has an implied obligation to reimburse the person who actually paid the money.

> *Example:* John Doe bought a business from Sam Smith. There were certain outstanding debts of the business. Doe had to pay off the creditors of the business. Smith had an implied contract to indemnify John Doe for the amount he had to pay Sam Smith's creditors.

indenture. A DEED to which two or more persons are signatories.

independent contractor. The basic test of whether a person is an independent contractor or an *employee* is by determining whether or not that person has the right to control the means by which his own work is accomplished. If he does have this right, he is an independent contractor. The question whether a person is an employee or an independent contractor may be important in law and may be hotly contested. An employee in WORKMEN'S COMPENSATION cases is paid certain benefits according to law, whereas an independent contractor is not. An employer is liable for the acts of his employees in NEGLIGENCE, but not for the acts of an independent contractor.

indictment. A legal written accusation of a crime, made by a GRAND JURY. An indictment consists of a heading, the name of the court, and the term of the court, the accusation by the grand jury, the signatures of the jury foreman or the members of the grand jury, etc.

indigent. Poor.

indorse (endorse). Literally, "on the back of"; to sign on the back of a NEGOTIABLE instrument such as a note or a check in order to transfer title of ownership to the instrument. Unless a term of QUALIFIED IN-

DORSEMENT, such as WITHOUT RECOURSE, is added, the indorser becomes secondarily liable for the payment of the negotiable instrument: That is, if the maker of the instrument does not pay it, the indorser is obligated to.

Example: Michael Smith gives his promissory note to John Doe for $500, payable in 6 months. In one month Doe needs some money. He goes to his friend, Henry Brown. He transfers the note to Brown for $400 cash. Brown buys the note, knowing that Smith is good for $500. All that Doe does to get the $400 from Brown is to give Smith the note with Doe's name signed on the reverse side. That means that Doe has indorsed the note to Henry Brown and transferred title to him. If Smith does not pay the note when it becomes due, Doe must pay it.

infant. In law a person who has not reached *legal age*—the *age of majority* as fixed by state law. Majority used to mean age twenty-one; but now most states have lowered the age to eighteen.

Infants, or *minors,* are a special concern of the state. Of course, if parents are alive and available, they normally have custody and control of their own children. When an infant is deprived of the custody of his own parents, the question of legal custody arises.

Generally, an infant does not have the same rights as an adult to do certain things, such as to make contracts, to sell property, incur debts, or generally handle business affairs. Some courts hold that contracts of an infant are voidable but may be ratified by the infant after he reaches majority.

information. An accusation made by some individual in connection with a criminal offense. Formal accusations are made by a GRAND JURY in the form of an INDICTMENT, but sometimes a police officer or individual may make a criminal accusation in an information.

Example: John Smith hits Robert Roe in the nose, breaking it. Roe goes to the district attorney's office and signs an information charging Smith with ASSAULT AND BATTERY. On the strength of the information, the district attorney advises the police and has a warrant issued for the arrest of Smith.

information and belief. A phrase in legal documents to indicate that the person executing the document does not know certain facts of his own knowledge, but has good reason to believe a statement of those facts made by some other person. Good practice requires that the person making the statement upon information and belief state the grounds or basis for such information and belief.

informer. A person who tells the police or other public authorities of the suspected violation of some criminal law. The informer may give the public authorities information as to the law violation, or may simply say that certain circumstances indicate that another person has committed a crime.

infra. A word frequently used in legal writing, meaning "below" or "that which follows." See SUPRA.

infringement. Violation of rights. The word is frequently used in connection with rights to a PATENT, or TRADEMARK, or in COPYRIGHT LAW.

ingress, egress, and regress. The right to respectively enter, go out from, and return from certain property.

inherit. 1. To acquire something from an estate of a deceased person by reason of a DEVISE or BEQUEST in a will. **2.** To receive something from the estate of a deceased person by operation of law when there is no will.

injunction. A court order, either commanding that an act be performed (a *mandatory injunction*) or forbidding an act about to be performed (a *prohibitory injunction,* also known as a *stay* or a *restraining order*). An action to obtain an injunction or an application for an injunction generally asks for a permanent injunction, one which will last for a long time. There is also what is known as a *temporary injunction* or a *temporary restraining order* (called a T.R.O.) to preserve the STATUS QUO pending the final decision as to the permanent injunction. T.R.O.s are generally not granted until after a notice and a hearing.

An injunction is a remedy in EQUITY, and it will not be granted where there is what is called an *adequate remedy at law.* For example, an injunction will not be issued for LIBEL or SLANDER, because the injured person may sue the wrongdoer for DAMAGES. Sometimes, though not generally, a BOND must be given the person against whom an injunction is issued. It is given to protect that person from loss in case it is eventually decided that the injunction should not have been issued.

injury. Harm done to a person, property, or to legal rights.

innocent purchaser. A person who acquires an interest in property without knowledge of any defect in the seller's TITLE.

innocent until proven guilty. See PRESUMPTION OF INNOCENCE.

inns and hotels. Places offering public accommodations for lodgings and entertainment. Proprietors of inns and hotels have special duties with reference to their guests and other persons whom they accommodate.

States, cities, and other political subdivisions have power to regulate inns, hotels, and other places of public accommodation with a view to protecting the public. Such regulations relate, among other things, to the construction of buildings, requirements for certain equipment and appliances, sanitary conditions, fire ordinances, the number of people accommodated, and the rates to be charged.

The law says that an innkeeper, hotel company, or proprietor of a place of accommodation must use CARE to prevent INJURY to the guests.

An innkeeper or proprietor of a motel is liable for any loss or damage to property of guests caused by his neglect or that of his employees. In many states a hotel keeper may limit his liability by giving notice to guests that he maintains a safe for cash, jewelry, or other valuables, and that if the guests do not avail themselves of the hotel safe, the hotel is not liable for loss of or damage to cash or jewelry.

Inns of Court. Institutions in London, England, to which persons go to become trained as BARRISTERS. They are known as the Inner Temple, Middle Temple, Lincoln's Inn, and Gray's Inn. They were founded in the fourteenth century and are much respected in England. Barristers may also have their offices in inns of court.

inquest. A legal inquiry. An inquest may, for example, be conducted by a jury to determine the amount of DAMAGES in a case where a defendant has DEFAULTed. The most common form of inquest is an investigation to determine the cause of a person's death; this is called a CORONER's *inquest.*

insanity. Basically, unsoundness or disorder of mind. Insanity affects many people in various legal situations. In criminal law insanity may be a defense to a criminal charge, because the law says that in certain situations an insane person may not be mentally capable of distinguishing between right and wrong, or be incapable of acting on the knowledge if he can distinguish between them, and hence not responsible for the crime committed.

In civil matters, insanity may render invalid the performance of certain acts, such as making wills and gifts, entering into contracts, conveying real estate, giving mortgages, etc.

insolvency. 1. Inability of an individual or a corporation to pay debts as they become due. **2.** Excess of an individual's or a corporation's debts over assets. Bankruptcy is another story; that is a formal legal proceeding. A debtor may be insolvent but not formally adjudicated a BANKRUPT. See BANKRUPTCY LAWS.

instanter. Instantly. In litigation, when a party is directed to do something instanter, he must do so at once. Sometimes a prisoner is directed by the court to plead guilty or not guilty instanter to a criminal charge; he must do so immediately.

instruction. In connection with a trial, an explanation given by a judge to the jury concerning the law to be applied to the particular case. The judge's instruction is also called a *charge to the jury.*

instrument. In law, generally any formal document in writing.

insurable interest. A pecuniary interest in property covered by an insurance policy, on which the company would pay if there were a loss or a death. Before an insurance company will issue such a policy, the prospective insured must show that he has such an interest.

insurance. A contract by which an insurance company agrees to reimburse a party for a particular kind of loss or to pay benefit or benefits upon the happening of a particular event. There are many kinds of insurance; in fact for high enough premiums, anything can be insured (even a pianist's fingers). The following are some examples of typical kinds of insurance:

Accident insurance (loss due to an accidental injury or death)
Boiler insurance (loss caused by a steam boiler)
Casualty insurance (loss due to an accident)
Collision insurance (damage to a motor vehicle colliding with some object)
Credit insurance (guaranty against bad debts)
Tornado insurance (loss due to violent storms)
Disability insurance (loss of earning capacity)
Fidelity insurance (loss resulting from dishonesty of employees)
Fire insurance (damage to property caused by fire)
Health insurance (medical expenses and loss of time due to illness)
Liability insurance (liability resulting from an accident)
Life insurance (payable to a designated beneficiary on the death of an insured person)
Marine insurance (loss resulting from perils of the sea)
Plate glass insurance (loss due to injury of plate glass)
Rent insurance (generally issued to landlords to protect against loss of rents)
Sprinkler insurance (loss, as water damage, caused by a sprinkler system)
Title insurance (loss due to defects in title to real estate)

A state may make laws regulating the conduct of insurance business within its borders. Most states have insurance departments that supervise insurance business within the state.

An insurance company may be a STOCK company, which seeks to make a profit for its stockholders, or a *mutual company,* which distributes any profit to its policyholders.

The party that buys insurance and pays the premium for its protection is called the *insured.* The company that writes the insurance contract or policy and assumes obligations to make payments is called the *insurer.* The person to whom benefits under the policy will go is called the *beneficiary.*

As stated previously, insurance is a contract. The contract is generally called the *policy.* The insurance company writes this policy, and in case of any ambiguity the policy is construed against the company. Most people find it difficult to read an insurance policy because of fine print, which may contain clauses that free the insurance company from responsibility in certain circumstances. There is a tendency on the part of some courts to hold that any contract containing print so small as to be nearly illegible is construed adversely to the party issuing the contract.

insurance adjuster. A person employed either by the insurance company or the insured; the most common use of the term refers to a person employed by the insurance company to investigate, report regarding, and if necessary adjust the insurance loss.

insurrection. A rebellion against an established government in which there is more than rioting or mob violence: There must be organized resistance against established authority for such action to be considered insurrection.

integrity. Although integrity is not strictly a legal word, it plays a part in many legal situations. It denotes honesty, soundness of character, and moral principles. Integrity is most important in the discharge of FIDU-CIARY responsibilities.

intent. The purpose or design one has in mind while doing something. In law, intent can swing a court decision one way or another. Much depends upon the intent or mental operation of parties to a contract. In criminal law *criminal intent* is a necessary ingredient to constitute most crimes.

inter alia. A Latin phrase meaning "among other things."

inter vivos. See GIFT.

interest. 1. A share or part of property. **2.** With reference to a lawsuit, a benefit or LIABILITY that may result from the lawsuit, or a relationship to the subject matter of the lawsuit. **3.** Compensation for the use of money or a penalty for the nonpayment of DAMAGES.

interim. Meantime. For example, a court order issued to take effect while other proceedings are being held is designated an *interim order.*

interlocutory. Temporary and provisional. An *interlocutory order* is similar to an INTERIM *order.* For example, in divorce proceedings an interlocutory order may be issued but the divorce does not become final until the lapse of a certain time.

intermarriage. Marriage between members of different groups (racial, ethnic, religious, etc.).

intermediary. One who has no interest in the subject of a controversy but is employed to negotiate a settlement.

internal revenue. I've probably used these words thousands of times. I knew what they referred to, but for a long time didn't know the origin of the phrase. I wondered why the word "internal" rather than "external" was used. After a little research I came to the conclusion that "internal revenue" meant domestic taxes or federal taxes collected *within* our country, as distinguished from customs duties, which have an international meaning. Internal revenue laws are found in what is known as the Internal Revenue Code. Revenue from whatever source is necessary for the support of government. So, putting it simply, internal revenue is one form of federal taxation and is a major source of income for the support of our national government. Internal revenue laws include provisions for income taxes, estate taxes, corporate taxes, gift taxes, and excise taxes on the sale of various goods, such as liquors, tobacco, automobiles, etc., and services, such as telephone facilities. The Commissioner of Internal Revenue is empowered by Congress to administer internal revenue laws. Serving under the Commissioner are many officials known as collectors or directors of internal revenue.

Thousands of volumes have been written on the subject of tax law. It is a highly technical subject. This book does not attempt to deal with the many refinements of tax law; I leave that to the TAX experts.

international law. The branch of law that governs the relationships of nations to each other. International law started about the sixteenth century. Its sources are customs and usages, treaties, and the decisions of such tribunals as the International Court of Justice and the International Court of Human Rights. International law is also based on various diplomatic papers written over the centuries.

interpleader. A remedy that exists when two or more persons make a claim for property in the possession of a third person. In order to avoid conflicting claims and double lawsuits, the person who has possession of the property asks a court of justice to decide who is the rightful owner of the property. This procedure is called an interpleader.

> *Example:* John Doe died owning a two-stone diamond ring. Fred Doe, a nephew of John Doe, says his uncle gave him the ring during his lifetime. Jim Doe, another nephew, claims he owns the ring because it was given to him in his uncle's will. Fred Smith, the executor, who is holding the ring, brings an interpleader proceeding and asks the court to determine who is the rightful owner of the ring.

interpolate. To insert words in a document. To prove that such interpolations are valid, all the signatories to the document *should* indicate— usually by initialing—that they have seen and approved the changes.

interpreter. In court procedure, a person sworn to faithfully translate EVIDENCE given in a foreign language by a WITNESS.

interrogatories. A series of written questions sent to a party to a legal proceeding. They are also sometimes used where testimony is taken by a commission in foreign jurisdictions. A modern development in legal procedure is to allow the use of written interrogatories in all cases. This permits the asking of questions the answers to which would not normally be used on the trial of a case, such as whether or not a person is insured, the name of the insurance company, whether settlement negotiations are in the process, etc.

interstate. Between different states of the United States. The term may become important in determining whether the matter in controversy is controlled by federal laws or state laws.

Examples of federal laws governing labor-management relations that apply to companies in matters involving interstate actions are the Wagner Act and the Taft-Hartley Act. The National Labor Relations Board administers those federal laws and has jurisdiction over labor matters that directly or indirectly involve interstate matters. See LABOR RELATIONS LAW. Matters that are purely INTRASTATE, such as the affairs of a local transportation company or a local merchant doing no interstate business, are handled by state labor relations boards.

interstate commerce. See COMMERCE.

Interstate Commerce Commission (I.C.C.). A federal administrative agency, now comprising eleven members appointed by the president, to regulate interstate commerce.

intervene. To come in or ask to come in and be a party to a lawsuit.

intestate. A person who dies leaving no valid will or testament.

intrastate. Carried on completely within the borders of a particular state of the United States. See INTERSTATE.

invalid. Contrary to law or lacking legal authority.

invent. In patent law, to create for the first time or discover. See PATENT RIGHT.

I.O.U. An abbreviation (derived from the pronunciation of "I owe you") that refers to a memorandum stating that one person owes another person a certain sum of money. See PROMISSORY NOTE.

ipso facto. By the mere happening of a fact or act.

irregular. Not done according to lawful rules and practices; in other words, not "according to Hoyle."

irrelevant. A word often used in the law of EVIDENCE meaning that something is not significantly related to the matter in question or the issue.

irrevocable. Not subject to revocation: that is, final and not changeable.

> *Example:* John Smith makes a trust agreement with the Excelsior Bank whereby he creates what is known as a "living trust." In the trust agreement John and the bank agree that the trust thereby created is irrevocable; that is, it cannot be rescinded.

issue. 1. A question in dispute in a legal controversy. **2.** Lineal, or direct, descendants (children, grandchildren, great-grandchildren, etc.).

J

jail. An institution in which an accused person is held to await trial or after conviction for an offense. See PRISON.

jaywalking. Walking across a street between intersections and other than at a designated crosswalk. In some places jaywalking is a traffic offense.

joinder of parties. The uniting of more than one person as plaintiffs or defendants in a lawsuit.

joint adventure (joint venture). An enterprise undertaken by a group of persons to carry out a single business enterprise for profit. It is similar to a PARTNERSHIP, except that a partnership is a continuing entity whereas a joint adventure is limited to a single transaction.

> *Example:* Howard Smith entered into many long-term (50-year) leases of vacant lots in the city of New York for use as parking lots. Smith died. His estate decided to sell his long-term leases. John Doe, James Jones, and Samuel Roe decided that they could make some money by buying the long-term leases of the parking lots from the estate. They bought the leases from Smith's estate for $100,000 and operated the parking lots for six months. Then they sold the leases to the ABC Corporation, an operator of parking lots in New York City, for $250,000. Their joint venture in the parking lot business was financially successful.

joint and several liability. When several people sign a CONTRACT, NOTE, or bond and agree to be jointly and severally liable, that LIABILITY means that each person is responsible for the entire obligation. All the persons involved may be sued together for their contract liability, or each individual may be sued separately.

> *Example:* James Jones, Sam Smith and Howard Burke sign a contract to buy a building for $100,000. The contract provides that the three men are jointly and severally obligated to pay the purchase price of the building. Burke and Smith are killed before the building is purchased. The fact that they are jointly and severally liable on the contract means that James Jones is obligated to pay $100,000 for the building.

joint-stock company. An association of individuals who contribute to a capital fund and receive shares in proportion to how much they have contributed. It is a cross between a CORPORATION and a PARTNERSHIP, having some attributes of both forms of business but differing somewhat from both. A joint-stock company, like a partnership, goes into business for the purpose of making a profit. It differs from an ordinary partnership in that individual members can transfer their shares in the company without the consent of other owners of the other shares.

joint tenancy. The ownership of real estate by two or more persons whereby each has the right to use the real estate; on the death of one joint tenant, the surviving joint tenant or tenants take the entire property free and clear of any claims of creditors or heirs of the deceased joint tenant.

joint tort-feasors. Two or more persons who commit a wrong (other than a BREACH OF CONTRACT) and are all jointly responsible for the resulting injury. See TORT-FEASOR.

joint will. See WILL.

judge. A public official who presides over a court of justice. Depending on the jurisdiction and governmental district, judges may be elected by the people or appointed by a state governor or by the president of the United States. Some judges are appointed for life (but see GOOD BEHAVIOR), although most are elected for a specified term. Most judges have broad powers and wide DISCRETION in the exercise of their judicial duties.

A COURT is something separate and apart from a judge, but generally the acts of a judge constitute the acts of a court. In order to be a good judge, an individual must not only have legal ability, but also be honest, conscientious, disinterested, courageous, impartial, and independent.

judge-made law. A phrase that refers to law established by judicial decisions as distinguished from law enacted by the legislature.

judge's minutes. Notes made by a judge of important testimony and other developments in the trial of a lawsuit.

judgment. The decision or determination of a court of justice. There are various kinds of legal judgments, including:

An INTERLOCUTORY *judgment* (which leaves a final determination for the future)

A final judgment (which disposes of all the issues and subject matter in the litigation)

A judgment by confession (after a defendant confesses and acknowledges in writing his liability)

A default judgment (when a defendant who is served a summons in a civil suit fails to appear or answer in the action)

A summary judgment (granted on proof that the facts are undisputed and that therefore there is no triable issue). A court on motion may dispense with a trial and grant immediate judgment (summary judgment) for either the PLAINTIFF or the DEFENDANT.

judgment creditor. A person who has obtained a JUDGMENT against a debtor that will enable him to obtain the payment of his claim if the JUDGMENT DEBTOR has sufficient funds.

judgment debtor. A person against whom a money JUDGMENT has been rendered.

judgment roll. Whenever a judgment of a court is entered in the court records, there should be filed in the office of the CLERK OF THE COURT the SUMMONS, the COMPLAINT, the answer, and various motions and orders that were made in the course of the case, together with the JUDGMENT of the court. All these papers make up the judgment roll.

judicial. Having to do with a court of justice.

judicial administration. Management of the courts and the legal system. This subject is a broad one, but is one of comparatively recent development. Perhaps it started in 1906, when a young man named Roscoe Pound, later to become dean of the Harvard Law School, delivered an address to the American Bar Association on "the causes of popular dissatisfaction with the administration of justice." During the last seventy-five years scholars have studied and written about our courts and the causes of dissatisfaction with them; the administration of criminal justice; the problem of a free press vs. a fair trial; improvement in the method of selection of judges; judicial education; congestion in the courts; judicial ethics and the tenure and discipline of judges; pretrial procedure; court management; judicial conferences; improvement of the jury system; and plea bargaining.

judicial convention. A meeting of delegates of a political party from a number of political districts to select candidates for judicial office.

judicial district. A district from which judges are elected.

judicial notice. A means by which a court may recognize the existence of facts of common knowledge without making it necessary for a party to the litigation to introduce proof of those facts. See EVIDENCE.

judicial review. The process by which a high court (generally an appellate court) reviews proceedings of a trial court or other lower court. Judicial review may also include a review by a court of general jurisdiction of proceedings of a nonjudicial body or administrative agency. The latter is sometimes called CERTIORARI.

judiciary. That branch of government which functions through courts to administer justice. The unique feature of the American system, both state and federal, is that there are three branches of government consisting of (a) the executive branch, (b) the legislative branch, and (c) the judiciary.

judicious. This word sounds as though it referred to judges. Not so. It may be applied to any person to mean prudent, and having sound judgment, discretion, or wisdom.

junior. A person who is lower in rank or seniority; often the word is applied to younger members of a staff of associates in a law office.

jurat. A certificate of an officer (such as a NOTARY PUBLIC) that an AFFIDAVIT or other writing was sworn to by the person who signed the document. Sometimes a jurat is referred to as a "swear." It is often erroneously called an ACKNOWLEDGMENT.

jure. By virtue of right or law. See DE JURE.

juris. A Latin word meaning "of right" or "of law."

jurisdiction. 1. The authority of a court to hear and determine a legal proceeding. **2.** A legal system or territory.
    See also CONFLICT OF LAWS.

jurisprudence. The science of law, whose purpose is the statement of various principles on which law is based. True jurisprudence is continually seeking to modify and improve law.

jurist. Generally we think of a jurist as a judge, but technically a jurist is anyone who is learned or skilled in law.

jury. A body of men and women sworn to decide facts. Although there are several kinds of juries, the term "jury" generally refers to a PETIT (or trial) JURY, a fundamental American institution guaranteed by the Constitution. It generally consists of twelve persons, although some states have reduced the number of jurors to six for other than capital cases.
    Trial by jury goes back in England to the days of Magna Carta (1215), and the process was brought to this country by the English colonists. Ordinarily there is no right to a trial by jury in an EQUITY action, such as one for an ACCOUNTING, to change a legal INSTRUMENT, to issue an INJUNCTION, or for specific performance. In such actions the judge alone decides whether or not the plaintiff is entitled to equitable relief.

justice. 1. The determination of right or wrong under rules of law. Justice is the object and purpose of law. **2.** A judicial official. Members of a court are designated by statute as a judge or justice. For example, a member of the U.S. Supreme Court is known as a justice; a member of the New York Court of Appeals is called a judge.

justice of the peace. A subordinate judicial official who presides over a court of inferior jurisdiction known as a justice's court.

justiciable. Capable of being decided by a court of justice.

juvenile court. Until the twentieth century, problems of juvenile delinquency were handled by our general courts. Now there are juvenile courts, which specialize in handling cases involving young people (the age limit varies from state to state). The goal is not punishment but rehabilitation in an effort to prevent juvenile delinquents from growing up as criminals. See also FAMILY COURT.

K

___

kangaroo court. An illegal court put together by people who try to make it appear authorized by law, though in reality it disregards established principles of justice.

kidnapping. The taking away or holding of a person against his will, usually for gain in exchange for the safe return of the victim. After the Lindbergh kidnapping (1934), the crime was made a federal offense when state lines are crossed. See ABDUCTION.

kin. BLOOD relatives. *Next of kin* has a technical meaning: the person or persons who inherit where there is no will. A modern word used in place of next of kin is *distributees*.

"The King can do no wrong." A maxim that expresses an ancient principle of English law. The principle was the basis for the rule of SOVEREIGN IMMUNITY, meaning that no one can sue the government. See FEDERAL TORT CLAIMS ACT.

King's Counsel, Queen's Counsel (K.C., Q.C.). In England, a BARRISTER who serves as COUNSEL to the crown (that is, prosecutor).

"know all men by these presents" (sometimes shortened to "know all men"). A phrase with which many legal documents begin but which adds nothing to the substance of the document except a form of polite address. We have used the phrase for several hundred years and probably will continue to do so until lawyers realize that it is meaningless.

L

labor relations laws. The branch of law that deals with relations between employees (labor) and employers (capital). Disputes between capital and labor existed in this country in the nineteenth century, but it wasn't until the 1930s, during the administration of President Franklin D. Roosevelt, that labor relations law began to expand and take on a new meaning. Acting under the Commerce clause of the Constitution, Congress passed the *Wagner Act* that created the *National Labor Relations Board* (N.L.R.B.). This agency was given broad powers to protect labor organizations from *unfair labor practices* of employers. The N.L.R.B. conducts intracompany elections so that employees can select their own bargaining representatives (labor organizations, or unions). The Wagner Act guaranteed to unions the right of *collective bargaining* (negotiations leading to labor contracts covering wages and conditions of employment). Since many labor disputes do not involve interstate commerce and hence are not subject to the jurisdiction of the N.L.R.B., the various states passed laws governing labor disputes wholly within their borders. (These state laws became known as "little Wagner Acts.") The subject of labor relations is a very important one in the American economy, and has become a highly specialized branch of law.

labor union. An organization of employees that represents those employees in bargaining with an employer for wages and conditions of employment.

laches. A neglect or delay in asserting some right.

> *Example:* Jim Smith and Tom Brown are partners in a mercantile business. Brown acts as buyer and goes to the Orient twice a year to

buy merchandise for the store at wholesale prices. For 20 years Smith manages the retail end of the business and leaves the purchasing of merchandise up to Brown. Brown pads his expense accounts. Smith becomes suspicious and hires an accountant to audit Brown's expenses. He learns that Brown has falsified his expense account in the amount of $5,000 a year and really owes the firm $100,000. Smith sues Brown for the padded expense accounts accumulated over 20 years. Never before in the 20-year period had Smith questioned Brown's expenses. Brown says that each year he had told Smith the amount of his expenses and thought Smith approved. Smith may not recover $100,000 because he "slept on his rights" and has been guilty of laches.

landlord. An owner of property who allows another person to occupy the property with permission and generally for rent.

land-poor. In the position of owning so much unproductive land that one finds it difficult to pay taxes.

lapsed legacy. When a LEGATEE dies before a TESTATOR does, the legacy may be a lapsed legacy and become part of the RESIDUARY ESTATE of the testator. Some state laws provide that legacies to certain blood relatives do not lapse, but pass to the blood relative's heirs.

lapsed policy. An insurance policy no longer in force by reason of a failure to pay the premiums. .

larceny. The taking and carrying off of personal property without the owner's consent by someone who is not entitled to the property, with intent on the part of the culprit to deprive the owner of the possession of the property. There are many different types of larceny. One of the most common is shoplifting, the pilfering of merchandise from a store.

In general all goods and chattels can be the object of larceny, including coins and paper currency, animals (hogs, cattle, sheep, chickens, horses, dogs, and cats), documents, records, tickets, postage stamps, and automobiles.

There are various kinds and degrees of larceny. Although there are many refinements to the crime, the basic categories are *grand larceny* and *petit larceny*. The graduation of grand larceny into petit is dependent on the law of the state where the property is stolen. If the law of a particular state fixes the dividing line between grand larceny and petit larceny at $500, then if the value of the property stolen is $500 or more, the crime is grand larceny; below $500 the crime is petit larceny.

last clear chance (also known as the *humanitarian doctrine* or the *discovered negligence doctrine*). The doctrine that if a person negligently puts himself in danger, he may still recover for injury if the person charged with NEGLIGENCE had the opportunity to avoid the injury.

Example: Mary Jones drove her car onto a railroad grade crossing.

The motor of her automobile stalled and Jones tried unsuccessfully to start the car. At the time Jones attempted to cross the railroad crossing, a railroad train was approaching the crossing about 2000 feet away. Even though Jones was negligent in driving onto the railroad crossing while the train was approaching, the engineer of the train and the railroad might be held responsible for the injury to her and the damage to her automobile if the engineer had the opportunity to bring the train to a stop before reaching the crossing. The law says that there is a question of fact as to whether the railroad engineer had an opportunity to stop the train as it approached the crossing. If the train could have been stopped, that was the engineer's last clear chance.

last will and testament. The WILL that actually disposes of property at the time of a person's death. A person may make a number of wills and testaments, but they are not last wills unless they are in effect at the time of death. The phrase "last will and testament" is commonly used in a will because the person who executes it intends it to be his last will.

latent defect. In consumer law, a difficulty that is not apparent. A latent defect may be the basis of legal LIABILITY on the part of the manufacturer or seller of the article. A latent defect is the opposite of a *patent defect,* which is readily apparent.

lateral support. The right of a landowner to have his neighbor's land support his land in its natural state.

> *Example:* Jones and Smith own adjoining lands. Jones digs an excavation in his land closely adjacent to Smith's land. Smith's land caves in as a result of the excavation. Smith sues Jones for failure to give lateral support to Smith's land.

law. A set of rules of conduct and action that are promulgated by a ruling authority to govern a civilized society.

law of the case. Whenever a court renders a decision or JUDGMENT or rules on a law point, either on an appeal or on the decision in an intermediate proceeding, that decision becomes the law of the case, and parties and subsequent judges are bound by it.

lawful issue. A term used in wills or relating to the estate of deceased persons to refer to descendants.

lawsuit. See SUIT.

lawyer. A person trained and learned in the law; one licensed to practice law. See ATTORNEY.

leading question. A question suggesting an answer asked by a trial lawyer of a WITNESS. Leading questions are improper on direct examination of witnesses, but may be asked on CROSS-EXAMINATION or when the witness is hostile to the party calling him to the witness stand.

lease. An agreement, oral or written, between the owner of property (the LANDLORD) and another person (the *tenant*) whereby the landlord grants to the tenant possession and use of property for a period of time at a specified rent. Generally a lease covers REAL ESTATE (that is, land or buildings on it), but it may also cover other property, such as an automobile.

leasehold. The interest of a tenant in real property created by a lease.

legacy. A BEQUEST or DEVISE of property by WILL.

legal. Pertaining to law or done in a proper, lawful manner.

legal action. A SUIT brought in a court of law.

legal age. The age fixed by the legislatures of the various states as the age at which a person acquires full capacity to perform a legal act, such as driving a motor vehicle or drinking alcoholic beverages. Also known as the age of majority. Legal age varies from state to state.

Legal Aid Society. An organization formed to provide legal service or legal assistance to the poor.

legal cap. The type of writing paper made for lawyers.

legal consideration. The term CONSIDERATION is used in the law of CONTRACTS to mean recompense. Any consideration which is good and sufficient is a legal consideration.

legal defense. A defense to a lawsuit which is VALID and sufficient at law.

legal disability. A disability that prevents a person from performing a lawful act. The disability may be physical or mental. It may be due to infancy, intoxication, injury, or illness.

legal discretion. The exercise of any DISCRETION founded on rules and principles of law.

legal domicile. See DOMICILE.

legal duty. An obligation which the law requires to be performed.

legal entity. Something that has an existence in law.

legal error. See ERROR.

legal estate. An INTEREST in property which is recognized by law. See ESTATE.

legal ethics. The set of standards among lawyers that defines their legal and ethical responsibilities to the public, the court, their clients, and their profession. See ATTORNEY.

legal evidence. EVIDENCE, either oral or documentary, that is admissible in court according to the rules of evidence. See ADMISSIBLE EVIDENCE.

legal excuse. Some reason it is impossible to comply with a statute or ordinance, or with a rule of law equivalent to a statute or ordinance.

legal holiday. A day designated by a state or federal law for the suspension of business.

legal interest. The rate of interest fixed by state law as the highest rate which may be required by CONTRACT or COMMERCIAL paper, or required to be paid on an overdue debt. Legal interest may also be the rate of interest prescribed by the law of the state as a percentage of interest which will prevail in the absence of any agreement.

legal investment. A particular type of investment authorized by law. State legislatures ordinarily designate particular classifications of high-grade securities for investment of trust funds by fiduciaries, since such investments are less likely to cause loss of principal than investments in common stocks or speculative securities. Legal investments are not as important as they formerly were because the courts have established the PRUDENT MAN RULE, which governs in preference to so-called legal investments.

legal liability. LIABILITY that the courts recognize and enforce.

legal life estate. An estate created by operation of law, such as those created under agreements or wills.

legal name. A name generally consisting of a given name and a surname, or family name. However, contrary to general public opinion, a person may choose whatever name he pleases as long as it does not cause confusion or impinge on the property rights of another, and as long as it is not done for fraudulent purposes.

legal notice. A notice that is adequate under the existing requirements of law. Commonly, newspaper ads in fine print (which people seldom read) relating to legal subjects (as required by various statutes) are called legal notices.

legal obligation. Any duty the law prescribes.

legal owner. This phrase is synonymous with *owner.*

legal papers. In general, the documents used by an attorney and his client in working out the solution of a legal matter, whether it be papers relating to a lawsuit or a contract or a will.

legal possession. This phrase is synonymous with POSSESSION.

legal presumption. An inference which the law requires to be drawn from established facts. Generally, legal presumptions relate to the guidance of the judge and not the jury.

legal proceeding. Any PROCEEDING before an administrative board or before a court of justice or a legal tribunal.

legal process. Any INSTRUMENT authorized or required to be *serve*d on a person by law, such as a SUMMONS to institute a legal suit or a SUBPOENA to require the attendance of a witness in court.

legal remedy. A court proceeding, whether it be an action at law or a special proceeding, to redress a wrong. See REMEDY.

legal representative. Generally, a term designating an executor or administrator of an estate of a deceased person, or an attorney at a legal proceeding.

legal responsibility. The responsibility of one who is obligated by law to do something.

legal technicality. A term most often used by laymen to refer to procedure that conforms to law but which laymen feel has undue weight in deciding a controversy.

legal tender. 1. That currency or money a creditor is required to accept in payment of a debt. **2.** An offer of money to satisfy a legal obligation.

legal title. The right of ownership that can be enforced in a court of law; a right that is complete, requiring nothing further to make it enforceable.

legal wrongdoing. The invasion of another person's legally protected rights.

legatee. Generally, one who receives a LEGACY of personal property under a WILL. A person who receives a gift of real estate under a will is called a DEVISEE.

> *Example:* Mary Smith dies leaving a LAST WILL AND TESTAMENT, by the terms of which she gives $5000 to her friend, Sarah Jones. Sarah Jones is a legatee who is the beneficiary of the $5000 legacy under the will of Mary Smith.

legitimate. 1. Lawful. **2.** Pertaining to a child born in wedlock.

legitimize. To make legal. Generally the term applies to the legal procedure whereby a bastard can assume the status of a legitimate child.

lèse majesté. Any crime against a government, particularly TREASON. From the French "injured majesty."

lessee. Tenant.

lessor. LANDLORD.

letters of administration. A certificate of the probate court that a person has been appointed administrator of the estate of a deceased person and is empowered to perform the duties of an administrator.

letters of credit. See BANKING LAWS.

letters of guardianship. A commission authorizing a person to take charge of the person or property of an infant.

Letters Patent. See PATENT RIGHT.

letters rogatory. A communication from a court in which litigation is pending to a court in another JURISDICTION, requesting that the testimony of a witness in that other jurisdiction be taken and transmitted to the court requesting it.

letters testamentary. A certificate of a PROBATE court appointing an executor or executors of an estate and empowering him or them to enter upon the discharge of the duties of executor or executors.

levy (n.). 1. Seizure. **2.** In the field of collecting, a JUDGMENT to seize property and convert it into money.

levy (v.). In the field of taxation, to collect by legal authority or by force.

lex domicilii. The law of a person's DOMICILE.

lex fori. The law of the FORUM or of the place where a lawsuit is tried.

lex loci contractus. The law of the place where the contract was made or the law of the place where the contract is to be performed.

lex loci delictus. The law of the place where the crime or wrong took place.

> *Example:* John Smith, who lives in New York State, had an automobile accident in Ohio with Fred Brown, a resident of Ohio. Smith brought action for damages in New York State. The New York Court applied the *lex loci delictus,* or the law of Ohio.

liability. A broad word meaning legal responsibility.

libel. See ADMIRALTY LAW.

libel and slander. I treat these two words as one subject, although each involves a separate legal wrong. Both libel and slander involve the defamation of someone's character or reputation. Libel, on the one hand, is the publication of the defamation by means of writing, printing, or signs or cartoons that expose a person to ridicule, hatred, or contempt. Slander is expressed orally. Putting it simply, libel is written, while slander is spoken.

Libel and slander may impute to a person dishonesty, fraud, venereal disease, drunkenness, falsehood, insanity, corruption, cowardice, cruelty to children, draft dodging, being a spy, betraying a trust, etc. Generally, the implication of any of those things may tend to injure the person's business, profession, or employment, as well as family and social life. Of course there are some LEGAL EXCUSES for such imputations; however, the principal justification is the truth of the statements claimed to be libelous or slanderous.

> *Example 1:* John Smith writes a letter to a public official saying that Howard Brown murdered his wife but that he got a good lawyer and the jury acquitted him because of sympathy. Smith has committted the wrong of libel.

> *Example 2:* John Brown writes a letter to the editor accusing Lawyer Jones of being ignorant, lazy, and incompetent, and says that Jones has neglected his clients and spends too much time in gambling and drinking. Brown has written a libelous letter.

> *Example 3:* Sam Smith moves to Rochester, New York, and there opens a real estate brokerage business. Mary Jones recognizes Smith and writes a letter to a friend saying that Smith is a crook and has served several jail sentences. Jones has written a letter which would be classified as a libel. If, however, Jones can prove in court that Sam did serve several jail sentences for crimes, she would have a good defense to an action for libel.

Volumes have been written on the subject of libel and slander. Limitations of space prevent me from doing more than scratching the surface of this most important legal subject. See SLANDER.

liber. The Latin word for book. Sometimes old records in county clerks' offices refer to deeds or mortgages as being recorded in *liber* no. _____ , at page _____ .

license. A right granted by a government to do something which without the license would be illegal. It is in the nature of a permit. A license may be granted by the federal, state, or local government, depending on the nature of the license and the provisions of the federal and state constitutions. Congress or the state legislature may delegate to various branches of government the power to grant licenses.

> *Example:* Under various state laws, automobiles are the subject of licensing. First, the automobile manufacturer or dealer is required to register with the state; then automobiles and trucks have to be licensed according to various weights and classifications; then drivers have to be licensed—all of which steps require the payment of fees.

licensee. See GUEST.

lien. A charge against property for the payment of a debt or the fulfillment of an obligation. Ordinarily, the person who holds a lien has the right to have the property sold for payment of the debt. Liens are created by contract or statute. A judge cannot create a lien simply because it seems the right thing to do.

> *Examples:* A laborer or other artisan who improves real estate generally is granted the right by statute to have what is called a MECHANIC'S LIEN. A jeweler may have a lien for the value of his work on jewelry.

life estate. The ownership of property during the life of a designated person.

life tenant. A person who has the POSSESSION and enjoyment of property during his lifetime.

limitations of actions. Limits fixed by statutes as to the time within which lawsuits may be started. The state legislatures may pass laws extending or limiting these periods.

> *Example:* The State of Iowa has a 5-year statute of limitations for actions on contracts or mercantile accounts. Jim Jones had Sam Smith build an addition to his house for such amount that would be fair and reasonable. Smith's bill was $13,750. Jones said the charge was outrageous and wouldn't pay it. They argued about the bill for 6 years. Finally in the seventh year Smith sued. It was too late. Smith had waited too long. He should have brought suit within the 5-year time fixed by statute.

limited liability. Legal responsiblity limited by contractual agreement to a certain dollar amount. The liability of corporations is generally limited to their assets, thus protecting the individual stockholders or owners against individual liability. See PIERCING THE CORPORATE VEIL.

limited partnership. A PARTNERSHIP under which certain partners manage the business and one or more other partners contribute capital to the business and limit their LIABILITY to the amount of capital that they provide. Agreements for limited partnership must be filed in a public office so that the public knows or can ascertain the restrictions on the liability of the limited partners.

lineup. See IDENTIFICATION.

liquidate. Generally, in legal situations, to convert assets into cash, pay debts, and make payment of the remainder to those entitled to it; in simple words, to WIND UP.

liquidated. In law, usually referring to an obligation, debt, or damage that is definite, fixed, and certain.

> *Example:* Farmer Brown's cattle broke down an old fence and trampled John Doe's crops. Brown admitted he was liable, but disputed the amount which Doe claimed, namely $3000. Finally both parties agreed that the amount of damages to the crops was $2000. How and when the damages would be paid was left open for further discussion, but the amount of damages became liquidated—fixed—at $2000.

liquidated damages. Damages fixed by a contract to be paid in case there is a BREACH OF CONTRACT. Liquidated damages must be reasonable and have some relationship to the actual damages sustained. Liquidated damages that are not reasonable or not related to the actual damages are considered to be penalties and unenforceable.

liquidating dividends. Dividends payable by a corporation or business company to its owners on the sale of assets of the corporation or company and not as earnings of the corporation or company. Ordinary dividends are taxable income, but liquidated dividends are considered a return or partial return of capital.

lis pendens. A notice of a pending suit that is filed in the office of a CLERK OF THE COURT. The effect is to tell the world that property is involved in a lawsuit and if anybody acquires the property, it is subject to the lawsuit.

> *Example:* John agrees to sell Jane a farm for $40,000. Jane and John have angry words about some trivial matter, and John will not sell the farm to Jane, even though he had contracted to do so. Jane brings a lawsuit against John for SPECIFIC PERFORMANCE of the contract—to force John to comply with the contract and deed the property to her for $40,000. At the same time she starts the lawsuit, she files a *lis pendens* in the county clerk's office, telling of her suit for specific peformance. John, annoyed by the lawsuit, sells the farm to

his neighbor, Harry Smith, for $45,000. Harry took title to the farm subject to Jane's lawsuit, and if Jane wins her lawsuit Harry must convey the farm to Jane for $40,000.

litigant. A person who is engaged in litigation; that is, a PARTY to a lawsuit.
litigate. To carry on a legal PROCEEDING by a SUIT.
litigious. Prone to frequently suing in court or often involved in litigation.
littoral. Referring to land that abuts the ocean or a large lake. Compare RIPARIAN.
lives in being. Some trusts must be measured by "lives in being" in order to be valid. In a particular case, that means that the trust will continue during the lifetime of a certain designated person or persons.

Example: Tom Jones by his will gave the balance of his estate to the XYZ Trust Company as trustee to invest, collect the income, and pay the net income to his two children, Jim and Sarah, and his three grandchildren, Sam, Howard, and Charles, as long as Sam, Howard, and Charles continue to live. As long as they live, Sam, Howard, and Charles are considered to be "lives in being" which measure the duration of the trust.

local law. A law that applies only to a particular city, town, or village.
local option. The power of a political subdivision or government to determine a legal issue within its jurisdiction by popular vote.

Example: The State of New York at one time granted incorporated villages the right to restrict the sale of alcoholic beverages within their limits. The village of Podunk passed a local ordinance restricting the sale of alcoholic beverages to 3.2% beer. In so doing, the village of Podunk exercised the right of local option.

lockout. In LABOR RELATIONS LAW, the refusal of an employer to furnish employment to workers by wholly or partly shutting down the business. A lockout is a weapon used by an employer in labor disputes, just as a STRIKE is a weapon used by employees.
loco parentis. See IN LOCO PARENTIS.
log. A record of a legal transaction. In ADMIRALTY LAW it is the record of a ship's voyage.
long-arm statutes. Statutes passed by most states which allow local courts to obtain jurisdiction over nonresident defendants if lawsuits arise out of transactions originating in the state where the local courts sit. See also CONFLICT OF LAWS.
lost instrument. A document that cannot be found after a careful search. Ordinarily, the loss of an INSTRUMENT does not affect the validity of the transaction of which the instrument is evidence, but it does make it more difficult to prove the transaction. Sometimes the other party may

require an indemnity bond before he will honor his obligation to the party that loses an instrument.

Example: The Empire Savings Bank issued a passbook that showed the amounts deposited in the account and withdrawals and the balance on hand. John Jones had the passbook. He lost it. After a careful search, he could not find it. He asked the Empire Savings Bank to issue a new passbook to him. The bank was willing to issue the passbook provided Jones gave the bank an indemnity bond, holding the bank harmless from any loss which might result from the loss of the passbook.

lump-sum settlement. Settlement of a claim by a single payment. For example, if a claimant may legally collect WORKMEN'S COMPENSATION in weekly or bimonthly payments for many years, the claimant and the insurance carrier may agree on the payment of a single sum, known as a lump sum, which will free the insurance company from future payments.

M

mace. A highly decorated large staff, symbolizing authority and often displayed in legislatures.

magistrate. An official or judge who handles minor criminal offenses or preliminary stages of other criminal proceedings.

maintain. 1. In lawsuits, to maintain an action is to commence it and carry it to its conclusion. **2.** As used in leases the word means to preserve or keep property in good repair and to prevent it from falling into a state of decay.

majority. See LEGAL AGE.

maker. Legally, the person who signs a PROMISSORY NOTE.

making a motion. See MOTION.

malfeasance. The doing of any evil, wrongful, or unlawful act; specifically, official misconduct or unlawful and wrongful doing of some act under color of official authority. See MISFEASANCE.

malice. Basically, ill will toward a person, but sometimes such malice in law may be part of an unlawful act done intentionally. Malice may be called "implied malice" or "imputed malice." Often the law reads malice into WANTON or reckless acts that disregard the rights of others.

malice aforethought. A state of mind in which considered malice accompanies or precedes the commission of a crime; generally the term is applied to MURDER.

malicious mischief. In general, a willful injury or destruction of property.

malicious prosecution. An unsuccessful prosecution carried on without proper cause and with legal MALICE.

malpractice. Professional misconduct on the part of a professional person, such as a physician, engineer, lawyer, accountant, dentist, or veterinarian. Malpractice may be the result of ignorance, neglect, or lack of skill or fidelity in the performance of professional duties; intentional wrongdoing; or illegal or unethical practice. In the last fifty years malpractice lawsuits against members of various professions have become popular and prevalent, and malpractice insurance rates have become very high.

malum in se. A wrong or crime involving inherent evil or immorality. An act *malum in se* is inherently wrong according to moral law.

> *Example:* Gertrude Smith was the proprietress of a house of prostitution. She was arrested because her acts were contrary to statute. Smith's actions were not only prohibited by law but they were also inherently wrong. She was guilty of *malum in se.*

malum prohibitum. A wrong or crime which is wrong only because it is prohibited by statute.

> *Example:* Brown was the owner of a herd of Angus cattle. The law said that cattle owners were required to submit to the Department of Agriculture of the State of New Jersey samples of any meat they sold. Brown didn't submit his meat to the Department of Agriculture and was arrested. He was guilty of an act which was not inherently wrong but was in violation of a statute and hence *malum prohibitum.*

mandamus. A legal proceeding seeking a WRIT or court order compelling a public official or corporation officer to do his public duty. *Mandamus* proceedings may also be brought against state, county, or municipal corporations, against public boards, and sometimes against inferior courts.

mandate. An official command generally issued by a court or a judge.

mandatory. Constituting a command. There may be a mandatory statute, but the most popular use of the word is in connection with court IN-JUNCTIONS and means required to be done.

manslaughter. The unlawful taking of a human life. It may be intentional or unintentional. It differs from murder in being committed without malice and in being unpremeditated. (See HOMICIDE.)

marital deduction. In federal TAX law, that part of an estate that qualifies as a gift to a spouse and hence is not taxable.

maritime law. See ADMIRALTY LAW.

marriage. Legally, a contract between a man and a woman whereby they agree to live with each other as husband and wife. Each state has the power to regulate marriages.

marshal. An officer of a municipal or federal court whose duties are similar to those of a SHERIFF.

marshaling of assets. A procedure in EQUITY under which all creditors receive their due proportion of assets.

For example, if creditor A has a LIEN on funds or assets in the hands of a debtor and creditor B has a lien on only one of those funds or assets, creditor A can be compelled to collect his claim out of funds or assets which creditor B cannot reach. The doctrine is not an absolute rule of law, but it is a principle that a court of equity will generally use to see that justice is done among creditors.

mass picketing. PICKETING by a number of people in front of a place of business. Though unions have a right to picket, mass picketing may be restricted so as not to interfere with traffic.

Massachusetts trust. See BUSINESS TRUST.

master. In ADMIRALTY LAW, the commander (also called a captain) of a vessel. He is employed or appointed by the owner of the vessel and has complete charge of the vessel, its crew, and its cargo.

master and servant. Strictly speaking, this refers to an employer and his employee. However, the law is so broad on the subject that it includes contracts of employment, the duties and liabilities of employers and employees to each other and to the public, the whole subject of LABOR RELATIONS LAW, WORKMEN'S COMPENSATION, etc.

master-in-chancery. An assistant to a court of EQUITY, appointed by the court. A master-in-chancery is generally a lawyer, and may perform such duties as reporting to the court on the facts of a case referred to him.

material. Essential or pertinent or going to the merits of a controversy.

matrimonial domicile. The place where the husband and wife live together. Formerly, court decisions in divorce cases put a great deal of emphasis on matrimonial DOMICILE. Now it is less important in divorce law.

mayhem. The unlawful and violent INJURY of another's body so that he loses the ability to defend himself. Some state laws define mayhem as willful and malicious injury to the human body; in other words, a willful ASSAULT with intent to maim a person or deprive him of a body member.

mechanic's lien. The expression is misleading in implying that the person who is entitled to the LIEN or property must be a mechanic. That is not true. Anyone who simply furnishes material or performs other work that goes into the improvement of a building may file a lien for the value of such material or work. There is a time limit, determined by state law, within which a mechanic's lien must be filed. The time limit is usually three or four months after the date of the furnishing of the material or performing of the work. You can see that a contractor who furnishes work or material is protected, because if he doesn't get his money promptly, he can file a lien. The lien can be enforced, and real property of the debtor sold to pay it within a year or two according to state law.

mediator. A disinterested person who tries to bring about a settlement between two or more parties to a dispute.

meeting of minds. The traditional concept, in the law of contracts, that there must be a complete understanding between the parties to a contract and an assent to all of its terms.

memorandum. A brief record of a transaction or understanding or outline of some intended agreement. A memorandum in writing may sometimes be sufficient in law if it contains all of the essential terms of an agreement.

mensa et thoro. A Latin phrase meaning "bed and board." It formerly was frequently used to describe a matrimonial separation, as distinguished from a *divorce a vinculo,* which meant that the chains of matrimony were completely broken.

mental illness. A disorder of the mind that prevents a person from functioning in society. The question often arises as to whether a person is confined to a mental hospital as the result of proper legal procedure. Courts have held that persons considered mentally ill, whether criminally insane or not, shall not be confined to a hospital until they have been afforded procedural safeguards in commitment proceedings, including a proper examination and a hearing upon notice, and shall have periodic reviews of the need to keep them committed.

mercantile agency. An agency that gathers financial information and credit ratings of merchants and individuals and reports data to inquiring customers. Sometimes mercantile agencies collect bad debts.

merger. Generally, the absorption of one company by another. It is to be distinguished from a consolidation, which is the combining of two or more companies or corporations into a new company or corporation.

meritorious cause of action. A cause of ACTION which is good, sufficient, and valid.

merits. See DECISION ON THE MERITS.

mesne assignment. An intermediate ASSIGNMENT by which TITLE to property is transferred.

metes and bounds. The boundary lines of land according to the compass or surveyors' instruments.

military law. The law governing the armed services. Military law is set forth in a *Manual for Courts-Martial.* Constitutional objections have been made to this manual because of its vagueness, such as its prohibitions of "conduct unbecoming an officer" and "all disorders and neglects to the prejudice of good order and discipline in the armed forces." But United States courts have shown a deference to military courts in their reluctance to interfere in such matters. See COURT-MARTIAL.

milling in transit. A privilege granted by railroads whereby, if the railroad transports grain or feed ingredients to a mill, the customer may reship the milled feed without extra charge for the stopover.

mining law. A highly specialized branch of law that deals with the ownership and operation of mines. The whole subject of mining laws was developed in the early days of our country when gold, silver, and copper mines were being developed. Some of the same laws, with modifications, are still in force today. Federal and state governments have given great opportunities to private individuals to stake out claims to mines and minerals in public lands. Claims can be abandoned and then acquired by newcomers. Sometimes after a claimant files and stakes out a claim, he obtains a PATENT to the land by complying with a state statute; then he owns not only the mineral rights but also the land on which the mine is located. Or the owner of the land on which the mine is located may lease the land to another along with the right to work the mine and collect profits. This is called a *mining lease*. It may include the lease of land on which oil, gas, or salt is found. Statutes have been passed regulating the operation of mines and protecting the safety of workers and the general public; regulating drilling, fencing, covering, propping and supports; and safeguards against fires or explosions.

ministerial officer. A person whose duties are to follow the orders of his legal superiors and whose job does not involve the exercise of executive DISCRETION.

minor. A person who has not reached the age fixed by state law to become an adult. See INFANT and LEGAL AGE.

minority. The state of being underage.

misdemeanor. A crime less serious than a FELONY. A misdemeanor usually calls for a fine or imprisonment other than in a state PRISON or penitentiary.

misfeasance. The doing of a lawful act in an illegal, improper way. It is to be distinguished from MALFEASANCE, which is an unlawful act.

misnomer. A mistake in naming someone in a legal instrument. The term generally means that a subject is given a wrong title in a pleading, deed, or other instrument.

misprision of felony. The concealment of a felony, or the knowledge of a felony and failure to report it. It is a common-law term not generally recognized in the United States.

misrepresentation. A false statement. Misrepresentation is an essential ingredient of FRAUD. See FALSE PRETENSES.

mistake. Everybody knows what a mistake is: some unintentional act or ERROR due to misjudgment or lack of knowledge. A mistake can have legal significance, particularly when all parties to a transaction act under the same misapprehension. That is called a mutual mistake and may be grounds for setting aside a transaction.

mistrial. The cancellation of a legal trial because of some ERROR or MISTAKE in legal proceedings. Often when a jury cannot agree on a verdict, the result is called a mistrial; that is a popular but inaccurate label. See HUNG JURY.

mitigating circumstances. Facts that tend to extenuate or lessen the seriousness of something. Even though mitigating circumstances do not constitute an excuse for an illegal act, they may be taken into consideration to reduce the degree of guilt. Also called *extenuating circumstances.*

moiety. A part of something, usually half.

molest. To interfere with so as to cause INJURY to or seriously disturb another person.

money had and received. A form of legal action whereby the PLAINTIFF shows that the DEFENDANT has in his possession money that belongs to the plaintiff and asks the court to direct the defendant to pay it over.

> *Example:* Robert J. Jones loaned $500 to Bob Smith. When it came time to pay the loan, Smith made out a check to R. J. Jones. The check came into the hands of Ralph J. Jones, who cashed it. Robert J. Jones sued Ralph J. Jones, claiming that the money was paid to him by mistake and that the money really belonged to Robert J. Jones. His action for money had and received was successful.

monition. In ADMIRALTY LAW, a summons to appear at the start of a legal proceeding.

monopoly. 1. An exclusive right such as a FRANCHISE granted by a sovereign power to a person or group of persons to buy, sell, or use something. This type of monopoly is legal.

> *Example:* The city of Syrchester grants a franchise to the ABC Telephone Company to exclusively sell telephone service to the residents of Syrchester.

2. A condition produced by one person or group that eliminates competition and gives that person or group control of the market for a commodity. This second type of monopoly, which results in a restraint of trade, is illegal, both at COMMON LAW and by reason of federal and state statutes. See COMBINATION IN RESTRAINT OF TRADE.

> *Example:* The Excelsior Steel Company, the Pioneer Steel Company, and the Crown Steel Company make an agreement that they will not sell steel below a certain price. The three steel companies control 90% of the market. The federal government brings a court action against the three companies to compel them to break up their monopoly. The government contends, and is successful in showing, that the agreement between the steel companies was illegal.

monument. A physical marker used in surveying boundaries of land (see METES AND BOUNDS).

moot. 1. Undecided; unsettled. **2.** Of no practical importance, a subject only for argument or debate.

Law schools often have courses entitled "moot court," in which the students try imaginary lawsuits based on fictionalized sets of facts. These may be trials of lawsuits or they may be the arguments of app-peals. **3.** A case in court may become moot when the subject of a legal controversy is removed (a case involving ownership of a cow may be moot if the cow dies) or discontinued, or the dispute is settled.

moral turpitude. Inherent wrongdoing, baseness, vileness, or depravity.

mortality tables. Charts prepared by actuaries showing the number of years that men and women of certain ages are statistically likely to live. Mortality tables are often used in court in the attempt to prove the life expectancies of individuals, for example in personal injury cases.

mortgage. A pledge of property to secure a loan. In most states a mortgage is regarded as a LIEN given as security for the mortgage debt. In some states, however, the holder of the mortgage may hold TITLE to the land. Legally, such title given by a mortgage can be defeated by payment of the mortgage debt.

Instead of mortgages, some states use so-called *trust deeds* in the nature of mortgages, or what are called *deeds to secure debts. Absolute deeds* given as security for debts are treated in law as mortgages.

A person who owns the property and gives the mortgage is called the *mortgagor,* and the person who lends the money and holds the mortgage is called the *mortgagee.*

Mortgages may be sold or assigned like any other property.

When mortgages or interest thereon are not paid, the mortgagee may foreclose the mortgage. See FORECLOSURE.

mortmain laws. Laws in English history which sought to prevent lands from getting into the control of religious corporations. The objection was that once lands were owned by a religious corporation, it was as if they were owned by a "dead hand" (the word *mortmain* means "dead hand" in French).

motion. An application for a court order. In other words, if a person makes a motion in court, he is applying to the court for an order. There are many refinements of court procedure in making motions.

motive. Cause of or inducement for the commission of a crime.

motor vehicle. It is often observed that lawyers use fancy words instead of plain ones. As an illustration, someone commented that he never heard a lawyer say the words "auto" or "automobile"—let alone "car"—in a courtroom. The word always had to be "motor vehicle." Legally, a motor vehicle is any self-operated vehicle that does not run on tracks. So obviously the term includes auto, bus, motorcycle, taxicab, tractor (used on public roads); and truck. The federal government (in a limited way), a state, or a municipality may regulate motor vehicles on a public highway. The state government (not the federal government or a municipality) has the power to license and control drivers of motor vehicles.

municipal law. A specialized branch of law dealing with cities, towns, villages; their power and authority; and their officers and boards or councils. Municipal law covers such subjects as the right of municipal CORPORATIONS to enact and enforce laws, regulations, and ordinances; public improvements; claims against municipalities; assessment and collection of taxes; and public works.

muniments of title. A collective reference to all the documents and other evidences that establish a person's TITLE to real property. See ABSTRACTS OF TITLE.

murder. The intentional and malicious killing of a human being. See HOMICIDE.

mutiny. An uprising or INSURRECTION of soldiers or sailors against their commanding officer or against military discipline.

mutual will. See WILL.

mystic will. Under the laws of Louisiana, a secret WILL. A mystic will is put in a sealed envelope and presented to a NOTARY PUBLIC with a statement by the TESTATOR that the envelope contains his will, whereupon the notary writes a statement to the same effect on the envelope. The notary then signs the envelope and witnesses it.

N

N.B. An abbreviation for two Latin phrases: **1.** *Nota bene,* meaning "observe well"; **2.** *Nulla bona,* meaning "no goods," an expression which a sheriff or other judicial officer puts on an EXECUTION, indicating that there are no goods on which he can LEVY.

narcotics. See DRUGS AND NARCOTICS LAWS.

National Labor Relations Board (N.L.R.B.). See LABOR RELATIONS LAWS.

naturalization. The admission of an ALIEN to citizenship.

navigable waters. Waters usable as highways for ship commerce. Generally the bed of a navigable stream is owned by the public: that is, the state or federal government. All owners of land that adjoins navigable streams have certain RIPARIAN rights, such as the right to have water flow past their property free of pollution and in its natural state, and the right to use the water for domestic purposes or for any other reasonable purpose that is consistent with the rights of other owners of property adjoining the stream and that does not interfere with public navigation. An adjoining property owner has a right to have access to the water; the right to use the shore or banks; and the right to build and maintain piers or docks.

ne exeat. A court order (sometimes referred to as a WRIT) forbidding a person to leave the jurisdiction of a court. (Latin, "that he not go out.")

necessaries. An article or articles that a person absolutely needs; something indispensable to or required for the continuance of life according to one's standard of living.

negligence. Failure to use that degree of CARE and vigilance that ordinarily prudent people would use under the same circumstances. The word is one of the most commonly used terms in law. Over 90% of the cases on court calendars involve some branch of the law of negligence. Early American courts relied heavily on a FAULT system, which in some states has been superseded in automobile accident cases (see NO-FAULT). However, basic negligence laws still apply to other causes of accidents, such as those resulting from defective machinery, excavations, ladders, swimming pools, elevators, doors, escalators, floors, ramps, steps, snow or ice, rugs, carpets, scaffolds, hoists, and shafts. Negligence may be a failure to properly light an area; failure to give notice or warning of a defect; failure to inspect or repair, etc. Many categories of people may be held liable for negligence, including architects, engineers, contractors, property owners, manufacturers, machinists, doctors, lawyers, dentists, and laborers. It would be hard to think of any occupation that is not subject to a claim based on alleged negligence.

A claim for negligence could formerly be defeated if the claimant was guilty of *contributory negligence:* that is, if he contributed in some degree to the happening of the accident out of which the claim arose. Now, however, many states have adopted the COMPARATIVE NEGLIGENCE rule, which means that if the claimant is responsible for less than 50% of the negligence that caused the accident, he may recover damages less an amount proportionate to his negligence.

> *Example:* Suppose John Doe's negligence was 10% of the total negligence that caused an accident and Richard Roe's negligence was 90% of the total negligence; in other words, Roe was 90% to blame for the accident. Then Doe could recover 90% of his damages.

negotiable. Referring to the type of INSTRUMENT (such as a note, check, or bond) that may be transferred by simple delivery of the instrument with or without an indorsement.

new trial. A retrial in the same court where a case was previously tried. A new trial is generally granted by the court that heard the case in the first instance or by an appellate court. The grounds or reasons for a new trial may be misconduct on the part of the judge, counsel, or jury during the first trial; some ERROR of law committed; some irregularity or defect in the proceedings; a VERDICT or decision contrary to law or the EVIDENCE; or newly discovered evidence (that is, evidence not produced at the first trial).

next of kin. Closest blood relatives; persons who would inherit property of a decedent who leaves no will. Sometimes a distinction is made between the next of kin and heirs whereby next of kin inherit personal property and heirs inherit real property, but that distinction is seldom used. See KIN and BLOOD.

nisi prius **courts.** Courts in which cases are tried before a jury.

no-fault. This phrase refers primarily to two branches of law: (a) automobile insurance; (b) divorce law. Over 20 states have adopted no-fault automobile insurance laws. Legislation varies from state to state, so much so that the disparity in no-fault automobile insurance in the various states may cause serious problems to the automobile user who travels across state lines, and as a result a national law has been proposed to achieve uniformity. Under no-fault insurance the insurance company pays the car owners, passengers, and pedestrians for their economic loss sustained by reason of automobile accident injuries, no matter who was to blame for the accident. Generally, no-fault insurance does not pay as much as the old type insurance, but as a practical matter it generally means that every injured person gets something for his injuries.

In divorce laws, there is a growing tendency to allow divorces on the ground of INCOMPATIBILITY of the spouses or the *irretrievable breakdown* of the marriage. Such liberal divorce provisions are sometimes called no-fault divorce laws, since they neither blame nor punish either spouse.

nolle prosequi **(nol. pros.).** A Latin phrase used by a plaintiff or prosecuting officer to state that he has decided not to further pursue or prosecute the case.

nolo contendere. A phrase used in a criminal action by a defendant to state that he will not contest the case. It is limited to the particular criminal action and has the effect of a plea of guilty for that one action, though without the admission of guilt.

nominal damages. A trivial sum awarded to a plaintiff. Nominal DAMAGES may be levied to indicate that the plaintiff was right, even though he didn't suffer INJURY substantial enough for *compensatory damages.*

non compos mentis. Unsound of mind; INCOMPETENT.

non obstante veredicto. **(N.O.V.)** A Latin phrase meaning "notwithstanding the verdict." Once in a while a judge orders a JUDGMENT to be entered N.O.V. This may happen, though it rarely does, when the judgment was ordered to be entered in favor of the plaintiff although the verdict of the jury was for the defendant, or it may be entered in favor of the defendant where the verdict of the jury was in favor of the plaintiff.

non sui juris. Not legally competent to manage one's own affairs, because of infancy, insanity, etc.

noncancellable. Referring to a certain type of insurance policy that the insurance company agrees not to cancel as long as the premium is paid. I once had a noncancellable health and accident policy. The insurance company found the particular type of policy unprofitable, and it sought out its insureds and for various sums of money bought the noncancellable policies. The company paid me a few hundred dollars and I surrendered the insurance policy to the company.

nonconforming use. If the use of a piece of property conforms to a ZONING ordinance, such use may continue indefinitely. If the use of the property does not conform to the zoning ordinance, it is called a nonconforming use and may be prohibited by court order.

nonfeasance. The failure to do something the law requires one to do. It differs from MISFEASANCE and from MALFEASANCE.

nonprofit. Referring to an organization whose object is to do certain things or carry out certain objectives in a nonbusiness way and not for profit. Such a corporation does not pay any dividends. Compare CHARITABLE ORGANIZATION.

nonsuit. An order of the court entered against a PLAINTIFF who fails to prove a case against a DEFENDANT. It ends the case and prevents it from proceeding to a jury verdict.

no-par stock. See CORPORATION.

not found. A phrase sometimes indorsed on a proposed bill of INDICTMENT, to mean that the GRAND JURY didn't find sufficient evidence to justify an indictment.

not guilty. A VERDICT of a jury acquitting a person accused of a crime.

notary public. A public officer whose duties are (a) to administer oaths; (b) to take acknowledgments of deeds or other legal instruments; (c) to certify or authenticate certain documents; and (d) to perform other acts with reference to commercial documents.

notice of appearance. A notice by a defendant that either he or his attorney has appeared in court in a civil action.

notice of motion. A written notice stating that on a certain date a MOTION will be made in court for a court order. A notice of motion is used in most civil actions.

notice to admit. In a civil lawsuit either party may call on the other party, by notice to admit, to stipulate the existence of a fact or a document in order to save expense of proving it at the trial. If the other party refuses to admit the existence of a fact or a document, the party refusing to admit may have to bear the expense of proving that fact or document.

notice to quit. A notice given by a landlord to a tenant stating that the landlord desires to repossess the leased premises and the tenant is required to give up possession and remove from the premises at a date stated in the notice. The notice to quit may be served as the result of nonpayment of rent, breach of provisions of the lease, expiration of the lease, or for other specific reasons allowed by law. See EJECTMENT and DISPOSSESS.

novation. The substitution of a new contract to take the place of an old one between the same parties. The old contract is extinguished.

Example: John Smith owned a 3-family apartment house and made a legal contract with Sam Doe to do janitorial work at the apartment house for a salary of $75 a week. Smith bought a 5-story apartment

house next door and made a new contract with Sam Doe to act as
janitor for both apartment houses at a salary of $160 a week. The
new contract was a novation.

nudum pactum. A promise without CONSIDERATION (Latin, "naked pact")
and therefore unenforceable.

nugatory. Ineffectual, and sometimes INVALID.

> **Example:** The U.S. Supreme Court held that a certain act of Con-
> gress was unconstitutional. It is proper for a congressman to refer to
> that law as having been rendered nugatory by the decision.

nuisance. A legal wrong that interferes with the rights of other people to
enjoy their own property or comfort. It may be (a) an unreasonable and
unlawful use by a person of his own property; (b) a person's unlawful
personal conduct; or (c) behavior injuring another person. Basically, a
nuisance involves a vexation or annoyance. A nuisance may be public or
private. It is public if it affects the rights of a group of persons; it is
private if it affects one person. A mixed nuisance is one that is a public
nuisance and also affects an individual or a few individuals. A nuisance
may be atmospheric, in the form of noise or odors; or an obstruction to
light, air, or view. Other nuisances include dust, smoke, soot, fumes and
gases, noxious smells, keeping a dangerous or wild animal, keeping hogs
or pigs in a municipality, maintaining dangerous structures, running a
bawdy house, storage of explosives, running a gambling house prohibited by law, storage of garbage or sewage, or running a fertilizer plant. If
a person suffers damage by reason of a nuisance, he may ask for DAM-
AGES sustained, but in some cases an action for damages would be an
inadequate remedy. Hence under certain circumstances a court will
issue an injunction ordering the abatement or discontinuance of the
nuisance.

> **Example:** I once knew an elderly lawyer who on behalf of home-
> owners sought an injunction against the owners of a factory and
> foundry prohibiting heavy smoke, soot, and odors to blow into the
> homes of the plaintiffs. The lawyer showed by expert witnesses that
> the owner of the factory and foundry could eliminate the soot and
> odors by installing a modern sophisticated device. The court found
> that the factory maintained a nuisance and issued an injunction pro-
> hibiting the continued use of the factory unless it took corrective
> measures.

nulla bona. See N.B.

nullity. A void action, or action having no legal force and effect.

nunc pro tunc. A Latin phrase, literally "now for then," used in the case of
an order or judgment allowed to be entered into court records as of the

date when it should have been entered. In other words, when something is ordered *nunc pro tunc*, it is entered retroactively.

nuncupative will. An oral will. It is made before a specified number of witnesses by a person (in some states limited to a soldier on active military service or a seaman or marine at sea) in his last illness and in contemplation of death.

O

oath. An appeal to God to witness the truth of testimony or a statement. It implies that the person taking the oath asks God to punish him if his testimony or statement is not true. The form of the oath is prescribed by state statute or constitution. See SWEAR.

obiter. Casually or incidentally. See DICTUM for the phrase *obiter dictum.*

objection. This word is most frequently used in the trial of a lawsuit. A lawyer calls the court's attention to something that the lawyer on the other side has done which seems improper by calling out, "Objection." If the lawyer regards a ruling of the court as improper, he takes an EXCEPTION rather than an objection.

objective symptoms. See SUBJECTIVE SYMPTOMS.

obligation. Something that a person is bound to do or refrain from doing. It may be a duty imposed by law, by a contract, or from his or her legal relations to others.

obligor. A person who has obligated himself to perform a certain act or acts. The most common use of the word in legal practice is to designate the maker of a BOND as an obligor.

obscenity. Generally, that which is lewd, lascivious, or abhorrent to virtue and morality. The United States Supreme Court, as the protector of free speech and freedom of expression, has set up these tests to determine obscenity: (a) Would the average person regard the work in question (motion picture, painting, photograph, statement, publication, theatrical production, or literary work) as obscene? (b) Would the average person, applying contemporary and community standards, find that it appeals to lascivious interests? (c) Would such average person find that it describes or depicts the subject in an obviously offensive way? (d) Does the work lack serious literary, artistic, or scientific value? If the work meets these tests, it is legally obscene.

obsolescence. A word often used in tax law to refer to loss of usefulness. Obsolescence may be the result of a change in the art or the industry; of laws that prohibit the use of something; or of physical deterioration or dimunition of use. See DEPRECIATION.

obstruction. In most law cases this word used alone refers to a barrier.

obstruction of justice. Resisting, impeding, or interfering with a police officer; or putting an obstacle in the way of criminal investigation; preventing a witness from testifying; suppressing evidence; or otherwise delaying or hampering the administration of justice. In most states obstruction of justice is a crime.

occupational disease. In WORKMEN'S COMPENSATION law, a disease that results from the conditions present in an employer's plant or a disease brought about by a particular employment.

of counsel. A phrase used to describe an ATTORNEY retained to assist the principal attorney in handling a case. It is also used to describe a lawyer who serves in an advisory capacity to a law firm. Often when a lawyer retires from a firm, he may continue to occupy an office in the firm headquarters and serve "of counsel."

of course. Legally, meaning "as a matter of right."

> *Example:* Sam Smith is sued by John Jones. After Jones has presented his case to the court and jury, Smith is entitled to present his witnesses to tell his side of the story as a matter of course.

of sound mind. See SOUND MIND and UNSOUND MIND.

offender. A word used in certain statutes to refer to a person involved in the commission of a crime; sometimes the word is used to refer to a person who commits a lesser crime or misdemeanor.

offense. A violation of law. It may be a misdemeanor or some other infraction of a criminal law.

offer. In CONTRACT law, a proposal to make a contract. In order for there to be a contract, the offer must be accepted. The offer may be written, or if the contract does not have to be in writing, the offer may be verbal. See CONTRACTS and STATUTE OF FRAUDS.

office. Legally, a public position of trust and importance (e.g. that of a president, governor, mayor, judge, or sheriff).

oil and gas law. A term used to refer to a specialized branch of MINING LAW dealing with oil and gas leases and with problems of ENVIRONMENTAL LAW arising out of the exploration and development of oil and gas wells.

on demand. When asked for or requested. The term is most frequently used in connection with a *promissory note* payable on demand.

on one's own recognizance. See RECOGNIZANCE.

on or about. Approximately. The phrase avoids the necessity of a witness being pinned down to an exact time or date when an occurrence took place. The use of the phrase in connection with a time or a date is intended to give some latitude for slight variance as to accuracy.

open a case. To begin a lawsuit. Opening a case usually means making a preliminary explanation to the jury or court outlining the nature of the lawsuit and the questions that will be presented to the jury or the court.

open shop. In labor relations law, a workplace in which both union and nonunion people may be employed. Compare CLOSED SHOP and UNION SHOP.

open the door. If one party to a litigation introduces EVIDENCE on a certain subject which is detrimental to his adversary, later the adversary may complete the picture by introducing more complete evidence on the same subject. Even though normally the evidence of the adversary on that subject would be INADMISSIBLE, a court may allow him to present such evidence on the ground that the first party has "opened the door" by introducing a part of the picture.

opinion evidence. Testimony by expert witnesses as to their opinion or what they think or believe with reference to certain facts. A lay witness is not permitted to give opinion evidence.

> *Example:* A man breaks his leg in an automobile accident. The attending physician is called to the witness stand and is asked whether the bowing of the man's leg as a result of the automobile accident is permanent. The physician answers that in his opinion the bowing of the leg is permanent. The physician is permitted to answer that question because he is an expert. An ordinary layman would not be permitted to answer the same question.

option. 1. The right or power to make a choice. **2.** The privilege of purchasing property at a specific price and in a specified manner. Often a prospective buyer will buy an option if he has not firmly made up his mind as to whether he wishes to buy the property. The seller may then not sell to anyone else for the duration of the option terms.

order. A mandate or command. Generally, an order is a direction of a court; sometimes it is a decision of a court.

A *final order* is one that decides the lawsuit itself. An INTERLOCUTORY *order* is one that settles only some preliminary or intermediate matter in connection with the lawsuit.

ordinance. A rule of law issued by the legislative body of a municipality and having only local application.

ordinary. According to the law of some states, a judge who has power over WILLS and PROBATE administration. See SURROGATE.

original jurisdiction, court of. See COURT.

overdraft. In BANKING LAW, a check made out for more money than the maker has on deposit in that account. Some banks allow overdrafts and treat them in the nature of loans made to the depositor, charging interest at a prearranged rate.

overt act. An action leading to the commission of a crime.

ownership by the entirety. See ENTIRETY.

oyez. An archaic word still used in some courts in the United States. It means "hear ye" and is uttered by a court crier when he announces the opening of court. In other states the court crier says, "Hear ye, hear ye. All persons and manner of persons, let them draw near and give their attention, and they shall be heard."

P

P.J. An abbreviation for "presiding judge" or "presiding justice."

pain and suffering. An element of DAMAGES that may be allowed in a claim for personal injury.

par stock. See CORPORATION.

par value. As applied to stocks, face value. Each share of stock has an arbitrary, nominal, or stated par value assigned at time of issue. Par value is not the same as FAIR MARKET VALUE.

> *Example:* John Jones buys ten shares of stock of the XYZ Corporation, having a par value of $1000. The stock actually may be worth $100 or $2000 on the open market.

pardon. An act of executive clemency, exempting a person from punishment for a crime or possible crime. A pardon may be granted by the president of the United States, a governor of a state, or a parole board. Compare PAROLE, PROBATION, and REPRIEVE.

parent corporation. A CORPORATION that owns or controls the stock of another corporation, generally called the *subsidiary corporation.* See HOLDING COMPANY.

parish. In Louisiana, a political subdivision of the state corresponding to a COUNTY in other states.

parliamentary procedure. The rules and customs governing the procedure of legislatures or deliberative bodies. Most deliberative bodies adopt their own rules. If they do not adopt their own rules, they follow some well-recognized parliamentary rules such as Robert's Rules of Order.

parol. Oral or spoken as distinguished from written. A parol statement is expressed by speech only and not in writing.

parol evidence rule. A rule in the law of EVIDENCE that prohibits the introduction in evidence of any change of a written agreement by any verbal understanding.

parole. The release on certain conditions of a convict before the end of his term of punishment.

particeps criminis. A person who participates in a crime. A person is *particeps criminis* even though he was not present at the scene of the crime if he aided and assisted in its commission. A person acting *particeps criminis* is an ACCESSORY.

particulars. The details of a claim. We often hear about a *bill of particulars,* which is the written statement of the details of a claim.

partition. The division of property, real or personal, which is owned by several persons. Partition may be voluntary or it may be ordered by a court. Partition may be division of property among its owners, or the property may be sold and the proceeds divided among the former owners. When someone resorts to law to effect partition, the legal proceeding is called a *partition action.*

partnership. A contractual arrangement whereby two or more persons agree to form a business enterprise and divide the profits or loss of that enterprise. Each member of a partnership is a FIDUCIARY, and as a partner owes a duty to the other partner or partners to act with the utmost GOOD FAITH. Each individual partner may act as an AGENT for the partnership firm. See LIMITED PARTNERSHIP.

party. A person or corporation taking part in a transaction or action. Usually a party is a person or a corporation playing a part in a lawsuit, either as a PLAINTIFF or DEFENDANT.

party wall. A wall standing between two buildings or on land owned by different persons for use in common by both property owners. Each owner owns as much of the party wall as stands on his land and has an EASEMENT from the other landowner for the support of his building.

passport. A document issued by a country's government certifying that someone is a citizen or subject of that country and requesting foreign governments to grant him safe passage.

past practice. See USAGE.

pat. pend. Abbreviation for "patent pending." It is usually seen on manufactured goods rather recently invented, and means that the inventor has applied for but not yet received Letters Patent. See PATENT RIGHT.

patent. The grant to an individual of some right to property owned by the government. In the days of European settlement in America the crown, and later state or federal governments, turned over to individuals large tracts of land by this means.

patent defect. See LATENT DEFECT.

patent right. An exclusive right granted by the federal government to an inventor to make use of or sell an invention or discovery. Under patent laws of the United States "any new and useful art, machine, manufacture, or composition of material," and "any new, original, or ornamental design for an article of manufacture" may be patentable. Certain kinds of organic life are also patentable; also arts and processes are patentable. Patent law is a highly specialized field, and some law firms handle only patent matters.

An inventor has to apply to the Patent Office in Washington, D.C., for the issuance of patent rights. Sometimes in connection with a patent application there is what is known as an *interference,* which is a proceeding instituted before the Patent Office to determine the priority of patent rights of persons who claim to be the inventor. An adverse decision of the Patent Office may be appealed to the Board of Appeals of the Patent Office. If the application for the issuance of patent rights is successful, Letters Patent describing the invention are issued to the inventor. A MONOPOLY to manufacture, use, or sell the invention for a specified term (usually 17 years) is granted by the Patent Office. Any use, manufacture, or sale of a patented product by anyone other than the patentee may constitute an INFRINGEMENT. An inventor whose patent rights have been infringed may bring an *infringement suit* for DAMAGES resulting from the infringement, or for an INJUNCTION restraining the infringement. Compare COPYRIGHT LAW.

paternity suit. A legal proceeding brought to establish the paternity of an ILLEGITIMATE child. Paternity suits are also known as *paternity proceedings.*

patients' rights. A fairly new development in law that concerns the rights of people committed to hospitals or other institutions because of physical or mental illness.

> *Example:* John Jones is committed by his children to a mental hospital, which confines and restricts his activities, though he is able to get to a phone. He phones his lawyer who comes to see him. The lawyer prepares a petition to the Superior Court for a WRIT OF HABEAS CORPUS. John Jones is brought before a judge who refers him to a physician. The physician reports to the judge that Jones's condition is one of senility and that he should be sent to a home for the aged rather than a mental hospital.

pauper. A person who is so INDIGENT as to have to rely on public funds or charity for support.

pawnbroker. A person who makes his livelihood by lending money on the security of personal property. The rate of interest charged by pawnbrokers is subject to public regulation.

payable. Owing to someone else. Most businesses classify certain accounts as RECEIVABLES or payables.

peace officer. A sheriff, a deputy sheriff, a constable, a marshal, a policeman, or any other civil officer whose duty is to preserve the peace.

pecuniary. Monetary. The term is used in some statutes that refer to monetary loss.

peeping Tom. A person who surreptitiously looks inside a house where people are living.

pendente lite. A Latin expression meaning "while a lawsuit is pending."

pension. An amount periodically payable to a retired person, usually by the government or a former employer.

per capita. A Latin phrase ("by heads"); often used in connection with inheritance to indicate that persons in a certain degree of kinship (BLOOD) share equally in the inheritance. (See PER STIRPES.)

per curiam. Latin for "by the court." An appellate court in publishing its *per curiam* decision gives the opinion of the whole court rather than of any one particular judge.

per se. In itself. Referring to a fact established without any outside proof.

per stirpes. A Latin phrase ("by stocks or roots") referring in the law of inheritance to a method of dividing an estate among descendants so that the children divide among themselves only the share which their deceased parent would have taken. See PER CAPITA.

peremptory. Definite, absolute, and positive, with no exceptions. A word used in connection with orders or commands.

peremptory challenge. Whenever a jury is selected, a party may ask that a prospective juror be excused without giving any reason. Such excusing of a juror is a peremptory challenge. Each of the parties to a lawsuit is limited to a certain number of peremptory challenges.

perjury. The act of making a false statement under oath. See SUBORNATION OF PERJURY.

personal property. CHATTELS or movable items as distinguished from REAL PROPERTY.

personal service. Actual SERVICE of a legal paper on the person required to be served. It is distinguished from *substituted service* or *service by mail.*

petit jury. A jury that tries civil and criminal cases and renders a VERDICT on questions of fact. It is to be distinguished from a GRAND JURY, which charges an alleged criminal with the commission of a crime.

petit larceny. See LARCENY.

picketing. A method used in industrial disputes by labor unions. It may involve posting union members at entrances to workplaces and displaying placards or signs or making verbal statements to persuade others from doing business with an employer. Peaceful picketing is lawful. MASS PICKETING, however, may be restricted so as not to interfere with traffic. See also BOYCOTT, which may be publicized by picketers at places other than the workplace. See LABOR RELATIONS LAW.

piecework. A method of paying workers by the quantity of work they do or the number of pieces produced, instead of by the hour.

piercing the corporate veil. Ignoring a CORPORATION as an entity and establishing LIABILITY on its owners. This procedure is sometimes followed to avoid FRAUD and ensure justice, but it is rarely observed because generally the corporate entity is recognized in law.

pitfall. A trap to catch trespassers on land. If the owner or tenant of the land does not give people notice on the land of the existence of a pitfall, he may be guilty of NEGLIGENCE and liable in DAMAGES for any INJURY sustained.

plagiarism. Appropriating the literary work, or a part thereof, of another person and passing it off as one's own work.

plaintiff. A person who sues, or otherwise initiates a legal proceeding.

plat. A map showing an actual or prospective subdivision of land and its features, such as lots, streets, and alleys.

plea bargaining. Negotiations between a person accused of a crime and the prosecutor whereby the accused pleads guilty to a lesser charge in order to avoid being tried for the crime with which he is charged. Although plea bargaining is sometimes the subject of public criticism, it is generally recognized as lawful and proper.

pleading. A statement in legal form of facts that constitute a PLAINTIFF's claim or a DEFENDANT's defense. The purpose of a pleading is to narrow the issues in a lawsuit and to advise the adverse party what to expect on the trial of a case. At COMMON LAW pleadings were highly technical. However, today in most states pleadings are designed to simplify the factual issues in a lawsuit. Pleadings may consist of a Complaint, a Petition, a Declaration, an Answer, a Cross-claim, a Counterclaim, a Reply, and a Bill of Particulars.

pledge. A transfer of ownership and possession of personal property as security for a debt, the property to be held by the creditor until the debt is paid. The person who delivers the property is called the pledgor and the person to whom the property is delivered is called the pledgee. Compare MORTGAGE.

plenipotentiary. A term used in international law to refer to a person authorized to act for another with full power in all areas of discussion.

plunder. Property unlawfully taken by FRAUD or without lawful right.

poach. To take game from another's land without permission.

points. Propositions of law or headings for an argument in a legal BRIEF.

police justice. A MAGISTRATE who presides at a police court and performs the duties of a JUSTICE OF THE PEACE.

police power. A term which refers not to the right of police to arrest people, but rather to the inherent authority of a state to protect the health, morals, sanitation, and general welfare of the citizens of the state.

> **Example:** The legislature of the State of New York establishes regulations for the pasteurization and refrigeration of milk. It has the authority to pass such laws by virtue of its police power.

policy of insurance. See INSURANCE.

political subdivision. A division of the state created for governmental purposes under a state constitution or statute.

> **Example:** The city of Rochester, Onondaga County, the town of Brisben, and the village of Smithville Flats are all political subdivisions of New York State.

politics. The science and art of government. (Many people today consider politics a shady word, implying tricks and artifices employed by people in or trying to get into public office.)

poll a jury. To ask the individual members of the jury to state whether or not the announced VERDICT of the jury agrees with the decision of each member of the jury.

posse. A group of people given temporary legal authority to assist in peace-keeping, searching for a criminal or a lost child, etc.

possession. Custody or control of something. It has been said that possession is nine points of the law. That saying is ambiguous, and is frequently misquoted as "nine tenths of the law"; but legal possession of property is most important. It may be actual possession or it may be constructive (legally sufficient) possession.

poverty law. The branch of law that deals with the rights of poor people and disadvantaged minority groups. The subject of poverty law has become a popular course in law schools.

power of appointment. Authority generally included in a WILL or DEED that gives a specified person, the DONEE, the right to designate another person or persons to receive the property of the person making the will or deed.

power of attorney. A document authorizing another to act as one's AGENT, either in limited circumstances or in general. See ATTORNEY.

precatory. Expressing a wish or desire. Sometimes it is important to find out whether a statement in a WILL is precatory or is a command or positive direction.

precept. 1. An order or mandate directing somebody to do something. **2.** A SUMMONS, WARRANT, or other PROCESS in criminal or legal proceedings.

precinct. A district marked off or set aside. Unlike a county, town, or other municipality, a precinct is simply an arbitrary division of land set up for administrative purposes. It is not a POLITICAL SUBDIVISION and has no corporate authority or governmental power. Examples are a police district and a voting district.

preference. In the law of debtors and creditors, or in BANKRUPTCY LAW, any advantage one creditor has over other creditors.

preferred stock. A class of corporate stock entitled to a preference over common stock in the payment of dividends and on the liquidation of the corporation.

prejudice. 1. This word is known in everyday use and is well understood as meaning bias or unfairness or onesidedness; the idea of prejudice is abhorrent to American ideals of justice. The word is frequently used in law to describe the state of a juror, judge, or arbitrator thought to have a preconceived opinion or bias. **2.** See WITH PREJUDICE, WITHOUT PREJUDICE.

premeditation. Prior thought. If a person premeditates a crime, it means that—even for a short time—he thinks the matter over and decides whether or not he is going to commit it. Premeditation may affect the degree of a crime. If INTENT is an element of a crime, premeditation may be deemed the equivalent of intent.

premises. 1. Lands or real property. **2.** Subject matter under consideration or previously discussed.

preponderance. In the law of EVIDENCE, the person who has the burden of proving a certain fact in a civil case must prove that fact by a *preponderance of evidence,* meaning evidence of greater weight than other evidence in creating the conclusion in the minds of impartial people that such fact exists. The rule as to preponderance of evidence is different from the rule in criminal cases; there the prosecutor has the burden of proving guilt BEYOND A REASONABLE DOUBT.

prerogative. A special privilege. The term is generally used in connection with the privileges of a high official such as a president, governor, mayor, sometimes a monarch.

prescription. A method of acquiring TITLE to real estate or an interest therein (such as an EASEMENT) by long-continued occupation and use. Compare ADVERSE POSSESSION.

presents. A written instrument; hence the phrase, which now sounds outdated and archaic, "KNOW ALL MEN BY THESE PRESENTS."

press, freedom of. See CONSTITUTIONAL LAW.

presumably. A word sometimes used by lawyers to mean that certain facts may be assumed to be true in the absence of conclusive proof to the contrary. In other words, "It is fair to assume that."

presumption for not testifying. In any criminal case there is no presumption of guilt of the defendant for neglecting or refusing to testify.

presumption of innocence. A fundamental tenet of Anglo-Saxon–American law: that a person who is brought to trial on a criminal charge is presumed to be innocent until proven guilty.

presumptive negligence. See RES IPSA LOQUITUR.

prima facie. A Latin phrase, meaning "at first view," used in law principally in two instances: **1.** *"prima facie case,"* meaning a case strong enough to justify a favorable verdict or decision unless it can be overcome by rebutting evidence, **2.** *"prima facie evidence,"* referring to evidence which, if uncontradicted, will establish certain facts.

primogeniture. 1. Seniority of birth among children of the same mother and father. **2.** The exclusive right of the eldest son to the real property of his parents. This rule had considerable significance in English law, but was abolished in this country by colonial and state legislatures.

principal. See AGENT.

principal and surety. The relationship of principal and surety is that between a principal, on whom rests some primary obligation to do something or to pay money, and the surety, who assumes the principal's obligation. The law of principal and surety is complex and full of technicalities. See SURETYSHIP.

prison. A building maintained by some branch of government to hold in custody persons accused of a crime or convicted as a result of a criminal proceeding. Some authorities distinguish between a prison, a jail, a penitentiary, a state prison, and a federal prison, but such places are basically the same in that they are places of confinement for persons charged with or convicted of crimes. Much study has been given by penologists and sociologists to the question of whether the purpose of confinement in prison is punishment or rehabilitation. There is a growing movement to improve living conditions of prisoners, and prison reform has become a special study.

privacy, right of. The right to be let alone and free from unjustified publicity. It is not an unqualified right, because sometimes the conduct or position of the person who claims the right of privacy may invite publicity.

privileged information (privileged communication). Information received between persons in a confidential relationship, such as information received between husband and wife, physician and patient, priest and penitent, and persons in a fiduciary relationship to each other. The disclosure of privileged information may generally be prevented by law. See EVIDENCE.

privity. A connection or relationship between parties to a transaction. There are many kinds of privities, but the kind that concerns lawyers most often is privity of CONTRACT, which is that relationship between two or more parties to a contract. It is necessary in law that there should exist a privity of contract between the PLAINTIFF and the DEFENDANT in a contract action.

pro bono publico. Latin meaning "for the public good." When an attorney represents a party without COMPENSATION, for the advancement of a public or social cause, he is said to be working *pro bono.*

pro hac vice. A Latin phrase meaning "for this particular case." Generally, courts will allow counsel who are not admitted to practice in the court's jurisdiction to act as attorneys on particular occasions.

pro tempore (pro tem). A Latin phrase meaning "for the time being," or "temporarily." Usually applied to a temporary officer, as *president pro tem.*

probate. Inherently the word means proof. In 99 out of 100 law cases the term means the act of proving a will to be that of the deceased person.

probation. A system of permitting a person convicted of a crime to go free with a suspended sentence, subject to the supervision of a *probation officer.* It differs from PAROLE in that it does not follow early release from prison but is a substitute for a prison sentence, contingent upon GOOD BEHAVIOR.

procedural law. See SUBSTANTIVE LAW.

procedure. The action a court may take to enforce or restore rights or remedy wrongs. It is sometimes referred to as *practice and procedure.*

proceeding. An ACTION at law. Whether a legal procedure is called an action or a proceeding depends on the language of a statute of a particular state.

process. In legal procedure, any document whereby a court, CLERK OF THE COURT, attorney, or other officer of the court requires the appearance of a DEFENDANT in court or compliance with certain orders. Commonly, a process is regarded as an order issued at the start of a legal proceeding to bring a defendant into court.

prochein ami. An old French phrase meaning "next friend." One who acts for someone else, as a person other than a guardian who acts on behalf of an infant.

prohibitory injunction. See INJUNCTION.

promissory note. A written unconditional promise to pay a sum of money at a specified time to the order of a named person or to bearer. Compare I.O.U.

proof. Evidence that tends to establish a fact.

property. See PERSONAL PROPERTY and REAL PROPERTY.

proprietary. Relating to ownership. *Proprietary rights* are the rights of the owner of property.

prosecutor. In criminal law, the person who initiates a PROCEEDING. The DISTRICT ATTORNEY is sometimes referred to as the prosecutor.

protest. In the law of BILLS AND NOTES, the certificate of a NOTARY PUBLIC attesting the fact that a note, check, or other negotiable instrument has been presented for payment and that payment has been refused.

prothonotary. The title given in some states to a CLERK OF THE COURT. He performs the duties of a county clerk.

province of the jury. Appropriate sphere for the jury's consideration. In law cases a trial jury is the complete arbiter of the facts in the case. Sometimes testimony or action by a court or attorney may be labeled as an invasion of the province of the jury.

proximate cause. That cause which in unbroken sequence and without the intervention of any other cause produces an event and without which it would not have occurred. Many times I have heard a judge charge a jury as to the meaning of the term and wondered whether the jury understood the legal definition. In everyday language I think it might be preferable to define the term proximate cause as the *real cause* of an event or injury, or the most direct cause.

proxy. A person authorized by another to represent him, for example to act or vote in his place at a meeting. The document appointing a person as proxy is also called a proxy.

prudent man rule. A rule of investment management that requires a FIDUCIARY to make investments with that degree of vigilance and prudence which a reasonable and intelligent man would use with his own property. Under the prudent man rule a fiduciary is not an insurer or guarantor of the funds he invests, but he is required to use the CARE and prudence that take into consideration the regularity of income desired and the preservation of the principal or the funds invested.

public policy. This phrase is hard to define. In general it refers to fundamental plans of justice, law, and order that prevail in a particular jurisdiction.

public utility. A business entity (generally a CORPORATION) that supplies the public with some service or commodity, such as telephone or telegraph service, gas, electricity, or bus or train service. Most states have public utility or public service commissions, which have the power to regulate the business of public utilities, set rates and charges, grant franchises, and prescribe what service and utilities shall be furnished.

publication. In the law of LIBEL AND SLANDER, the making of a slanderous or libelous statement to some person other than the person who is defamed.

punitive damages. See DAMAGES.

purchase money mortgage. A MORTGAGE given at the time real estate is purchased as part of the purchase price.

Q
_____

qualified. Of course the word qualified means competent or capable, but most frequently in law the word is used in connection with a plan that has been approved by a government office, such as the Internal Revenue Service. The word also is frequently used in law to indicate that a person filling a public office has taken the necessary steps to take office, such as giving a bond or taking an oath.

qualified indorsement (endorsement) An indorsement of a negotiable instrument whereby the indorser restricts his LIABILITY as an indorser. Generally the term WITHOUT RECOURSE is used to restrict that liability. In order for a person holding a negotiable instrument to transfer that instrument to another person, the holder must INDORSE the instrument. Ordinarily—that is, without a term of qualified indorsement—the result of an indorsement is to impose liability on the indorser.

quantum meruit. A Latin phrase meaning "as much as he deserves." It was used in ancient PLEADING when a person suing for payment for work or services was unable to prove the existence of a contract. He could, however, recover for the actual value of the services or work on the theory that he was entitled to as much as he deserved.

quare clausum fregit. A Latin phrase meaning "wherefore he broke the close." It was used in ancient times to describe an action in trespass to recover DAMAGES for the unlawful entry upon another's land.

quash. To annul or make VOID.

   Example: When I practiced law in New York State, I once took the testimony of a witness by DEPOSITION. There was a New York court rule which said that every witness must sign his deposition. The witness died without having signed. My adversary made a motion for an order to quash the deposition because the witness had not signed it. The judge quashed the deposition.

quasi. A word from the Latin for "as if." Used with a noun it means that the subject resembles the noun. The word in law has the meaning that something is almost the same as or analogous to another subject.

> **Example:** A quasi contract is an arrangement technically not a contract but creating obligations similar to contractual obligations.

query. Question. In law the word is often used with a synopsis or digest of a reported court case, to indicate that there is some doubt as to the rule stated by the case.

quid pro quo. A Latin phrase meaning a fair exchange (literally, "something for something"). In the law of contracts the phrase is often used to mean adequate CONSIDERATION for a contract.

quieting title. In general, an action brought in court to determine adverse claims to property.

quietus. That which silences a claim or discharges a debt for all time.

quitclaim deed. The weakest kind of a DEED. All that a person does when he signs a quitclaim deed is to convey any INTEREST he may have in a particular piece of property. He does not warrant or guarantee TITLE to the land in question.

quittance. A receipt or release. (Technically an abbreviation of *acquittance.*)

quo warranto. A proceeding in court to test the validity of a public office or a FRANCHISE.

quorum. The number of members of any deliberative or other membership body required for the legal transaction of business.

quotation. In a law BRIEF, whenever the exact language of a statute or court decision is set forth, it is called a quotation. Compare CITATION (2).

R

railroad law. A branch of law that includes rules for the acquisition of RIGHT OF WAY; the construction, maintenance, and operation of railroad equipment; the LIABILITY of railroads for accidents at highway crossings, for injuries to humans and animals, for fires, for injuries to LICENSEES or trespassers on railroad premises, and for labor, material, and supplies; CONTRACTS for the control, operation, and use of railroads; the issuance of railroad SECURITIES; the operation of railroad stations and other facilities; the ABANDONMENT of railroad lines; the consolidation and merger of railroads. Because railroads played such an important part in the development of our country, it was natural that a good deal of law developed to regulate the organization, development, and functioning of railroads.

rape. Forcible sexual intercourse against the will of a woman. *Statutory rape* is sexual intercourse with any female child under a specified age (fixed by state law), with or without her consent.

re. See IN RE.

real action. An ACTION brought for the recovery of REAL ESTATE. This procedure has been largely succeeded by other legal remedies.

real estate. Property in land and buildings.

real property. Interest in land and whatever is attached to it that is not readily moveable. Distinguished from PERSONAL PROPERTY.

realty. See REAL ESTATE.

reasonable. Of course reasonable means fair and proper, but what is fair and proper under specific circumstances depends on many factors. The term itself is elastic and flexible, and legally the word can be the subject of much controversy because it may involve disputed questions of facts.

reasonable doubt. That doubt which might prevent a reasonable person from accepting the truth of certain evidence. See BEYOND A REASONABLE DOUBT.

reasonable man. A hypothetical person whose conduct is a standard for CARE, attention, knowledge, and judgment to test the same qualities of a person involved in a lawsuit.

rebate. A return of part of a payment; a discount, deduction, or refund.

rebut. To overcome or contradict a preceding argument or introduce evidence or facts contrary to it. A word often used in connection with legal presumption, legal arguments, or legal briefs.

rebuttable presumption. Sometimes the law says that a certain fact is presumed to be true, but it may be rebutted by EVIDENCE or in other ways be disproved. That is called a rebuttable presumption.

recant. To withdraw or repudiate a statement—for example, a confession.

recapitalize. To change the capital structure. A term often used in connection with CORPORATIONS.

receivable. The amount or amounts a business is legally entitled to receive. Used in connection with ACCOUNTING statements. Compare PAYABLE.

receiver. A person appointed by a court to take custody of the property of another person or corporation while a judicial proceeding is pending.

receiving stolen goods. Receiving stolen goods is a crime, provided the person receiving them knows that they were stolen. "Fence" is the word commonly used to designate someone in the business of receiving stolen goods and helping the thief dispose of them.

recess. In court practice sometimes court business is suspended for a short period of time; that period is called a recess, not an adjournment.

recidivist. Habitual criminal; especially one who "relapses" into a life of crime after being released from prison as rehabilitated.

recognizance. An obligation entered in a court record, conditioned on the performance of some act.

   Sometimes we read in the newspapers that an alleged criminal is released by the judge *on his own recognizance*. That means that the judge temporarily releases the person without BAIL, on the strength of that person's undertaking to return to court whenever the court designates.

reconciliation. The renewal of friendly relations between persons who have been at odds. When married persons plan a divorce or separation, sometimes an effort is made at reconciliation.

record. See RECORDS.

recorder. In some states a recorder is the same as a MAGISTRATE.

records. In law this word generally refers to public or official records. Public records are those required to be kept in an office maintained by a branch of government. Legal documents are either *filed* or *recorded* in public offices. Filing consists of the delivery of documents themselves to the office that keeps and indexes them (for example, the office of a city clerk or a county clerk). Recording is the copying or transcribing of a document or its highlights in a permanent record book. State statutes prescribe which documents shall be filed and which instruments shall be recorded.

recover. To collect, to obtain, or to regain. In connection with lawsuits the term may mean to be successful in a suit or to obtain a favorable result or JUDGMENT.

recusation. Disqualification of a particular judge from hearing a case, by reason of his interest in the subject matter of the litigation or because of his PREJUDICE or partiality.

redeem. To buy back. It may also mean to free property from a pledge or a MORTGAGE. A CORPORATION may redeem its own corporate stock; that is called *redemption of stock*.

redress. See REMEDY.

referee. A person (generally a lawyer) to whom a court refers particular matters for findings of fact or decisions in the lawsuit. See REFERENCE.

reference. The sending by a court of a court case or some phase thereof to a person who thereby becomes a REFEREE to hear and determine the case or part of it, or to take testimony and report to the court. References generally are by consent of the parties, but in rare cases the court may order a reference without such consent.

reformation of instruments. An equitable remedy whereby an INSTRUMENT is revised or interpreted to express the real intention of the parties when some mistake has been made or a FRAUD committed.

reformatory. An institution for the rehabilitation of youthful criminals, sometimes referred to as *reform school*. State statutes provide for the establishment and maintenance of reformatories.

refreshing one's memory. When a witness in a courtroom does not recollect certain facts, that witness may be permitted to refresh his memory, and then testify as to these matters. The memory of a witness may be refreshed by oral statements or written memoranda, but these refreshers are not entered in evidence.

register. An official book in which public RECORDS are kept. It also means an official who maintains the register. For example, a register of deeds is an official who has the duty of recording instruments affecting real estate.

registration of land titles. Some states have systems that register TITLES to land. Under such a system, title to particular land can be definitely ascertained by reference to a public REGISTER.

rehearing. A second hearing before the same TRIBUNAL. Sometimes used interchangeably with NEW TRIAL.

relator. A person on whose behalf certain WRITS are issued and who is really the PLAINTIFF in the legal proceeding. If the proceeding is entitled *People of the State of New York ex. rel. Herbert Jones* v. *Smith,* Herbert Jones is the relator and plaintiff in interest.

release (noun). A term frequently used in law to mean the giving up of some right or claim. It may also refer to the paper or instrument by which a person gives up the right or claim.

release (verb). To let go or discharge or surrender a claim or right.

relevant. Pertinent, proper, bearing on the subject at hand. Most frequently used to describe EVIDENCE.

relief. See REMEDY.

rem. See IN REM.

remainder. 1. In the law of REAL ESTATE, that interest in property left over after an earlier estate, such as an *estate for years* or an *estate for life,* has terminated. **2.** In residuary clauses or WILLS, the balance of an estate after every LEGACY and DEVISE has been paid.

remainderman. The owner of a REMAINDER interest in an estate.

remand. To send back. **1.** A term used in law when an appellate court sends a case back to the court in which the case was originally tried, with instructions to take some further action. **2.** To recommit an alleged criminal to custody after a preliminary hearing.

remedy. The legal means of enforcing a right or redressing a wrong. There is an old legal saying that "there is no wrong without a remedy." Also called *relief.*

remise. To discharge or forgive a claim. Used in standard forms of legal releases.

remittitur. An action by an appellate court sending a case back to a lower court and directing its disposition.

removal of causes. The transfer of cases from one court to another. Often cases are removed from a state court to a federal court. Such transfers are authorized by various laws passed by Congress.

renegotiation. The review of government contracts by a government board or panel to determine a fair profit to be made by a wartime contractor.

rent. The amount paid by a tenant under a LEASE. It is compensation for the use of real estate.

reorganization. A term frequently used legally in connection with corporations; a *corporate reorganization* is a restructuring of that CORPORATION. It may involve the amendment of the certificate of incorporation, the amendment of the bylaws, and/or the issuance of new stocks or bonds. Usually corporations reorganize in the course of solving their financial difficulties. In fact, there are sections of the BANKRUPTCY LAWS that deal mainly with corporate reorganizations and rehabilitation. In cases of corporate reorganization, creditors of the corporation often become its stockholders.

repeal. To annul, cancel, abolish, dismiss, retract, or revoke.

replevin. The term for an action at law brought to recover PERSONAL PROPERTY wrongfully detained. Included in the action may be a claim for DAMAGES occasioned by such wrongful detention. The verb used in a replevin action is *replevy*.

reply. In the law of PLEADINGS, an answer to a defendant's counterclaim.

reports. The bound volumes of court or board decisions.

repossess. To regain possession of property, especially in default of installment payments due.

represent. To speak, act, or stand in the place of another person. When a lawyer appears in court, he represents his client.

reprieve. The postponement of the sentence in a criminal case. Compare PROBATION, PAROLE, and PARDON.

request to charge. At the conclusion of a court case tried before a jury, the trial judge instructs the jury as to the law applicable to the case. This instruction is called the CHARGE TO A JURY. Lawyers for both sides may request the judge to charge certain principles of law. These requests are called requests to charge. In some courts, requests to charge must be submitted to the trial judge in writing in advance of the charge.

res. The Latin word meaning "thing"; sometimes used to refer to the subject matter of a lawsuit.

res gestae. A term from the Latin, "things done," meaning facts relating to a legal issue. Something said may be admissible, even though it is hearsay, if it was part of the transaction which is the subject of the lawsuit and hence part of the *res gestae*. See EVIDENCE.

res inter alios acta. A Latin phrase meaning "a thing done among others." An act by strangers to the lawsuit.

res ipsa loquitur. Literally, this Latin phrase means "the thing speaks for itself." A doctrine in the law of NEGLIGENCE meaning that a person is presumptively negligent if the object that caused an injury was entirely under the control of that person.

> *Example:* John Jones has an apartment on which there is a balcony. Jones keeps pots of geraniums on the edge of the balcony. Sam Smith, a pedestrian walking under the balcony, was hit by a geranium pot that fell from Jones' balcony. Under the doctrine of *res ipsa loquitur,* Jones is presumptively negligent.

res judicata (res adjudicata). A Latin phrase ("judged matter") referring to a particular controversy that a court has decided and that is settled and shall not be reopened.

rescind. In connection with CONTRACTS, to revoke or cancel.

rescission. The act of rescinding or cancellation.

reservation. A clause in a DEED by which the grantor reserves a specific interest in the property conveyed.

residuary estate. That part of a decedent's estate which remains after the payment of debts, expenses of administration, legacies, and devises. The *residuary* LEGATEE is the one who receives whatever is left over after specific bequests and all debts are paid.

respondeat superior. A Latin phrase ("let the superior respond") that expresses a fundamental principle of law: that a principal is liable for the wrongful acts of his AGENT.

respondent. 1. A person against whom a petition is filed and who must file an answer to it. **2.** A litigant against whom an appeal is taken.

rest. To end. In a civil trial, you will hear the lawyer for a plaintiff say after finishing the plaintiff's case, "The plaintiff rests." In a criminal trial at the end of the prosecution you will hear the district attorney say, "The state rests." At the conclusion of the defendant's case, in both civil and criminal trials, you will hear the defendant's lawyer say, "The defendant rests."

restraining order (restraining injunction). See INJUNCTION.

restraint of trade. See COMBINATION IN RESTRAINT OF TRADE.

restrictive covenant. A provision in a DEED limiting the use of land.

retainer. 1. The fee paid by a client to an attorney for services or claims on future services. **2.** The act of a client in engaging an attorney.

return. A completed tax form, to be filed with the Internal Revenue Service.

return date. Whenever a legal notice or DEMAND is served, it may call for action on a certain date; that date is called the return date.

reversible error. A MISTAKE or ERROR made by a trial court which an appellate court deems of sufficient importance to affect justice in the case, so that a NEW TRIAL is required. Compare HARMLESS ERROR.

reversion. A person, upon signing a deed, may provide therein that on the happening of a certain event, or the expiration of a specified time, the property will return to the grantor or his heirs. The interest the grantor has in the property is known as a reversion.

review. The judicial examination by an appellate court of proceedings in a lower court.

revocation. 1. The recall or cancellation of a power or authority of an AGENT. **2.** The cancellation of a written instrument.

Richard Roe. A fictitious name (like JOHN DOE) used in legal illustrations.

right of privacy. See PRIVACY, RIGHT OF.

right of way. An EASEMENT to pass over another person's property.

riparian. Relating to the banks of a river or a lake. Often in law the term *riparian rights* is used to refer to rights of the owners of such banks, especially of NAVIGABLE WATERS. Compare LITTORAL.

robbery. The crime of taking property from another person against his will under threat of fear or force.

Robert's Rules of Order. See PARLIAMENTARY PROCEDURE.

S

S.E.C. See SECURITIES.

said. A characteristically legal word frequently used in contracts and other documents to mean "above-mentioned" or "aforesaid."

sale. A transfer of property for a CONSIDERATION, generally money. A sale may be a private sale following negotiation to fix a price, a sale of consumer goods at a predetermined price, or a public sale made at auction to the highest bidder. Evidence of the sale is a writing called a *bill of sale,* which passes TITLE to the goods in question. As you know, a retail sale of personal property is a sale of a small quantity of goods made directly to a consumer, while a wholesale sale is the sale of goods in bulk to a retailer. The law of sales is complicated. The Uniform Commercial Code (which has been adopted by every state except Louisiana) has many rules regarding sales, dealing with the time when title passes, the risk of loss where goods are lost or destroyed in transit, the warranties that go with a sale of personal property, and the remedies of a seller or buyer.

salvage. In ADMIRALTY LAW, the compensation allowed a person who rescues a ship or her cargo from the perils of the sea.

satisfaction. The discharge of some obligation such as a JUDGMENT or a MORTGAGE. The instrument evidencing such discharge is also called a satisfaction.

scab. In labor disputes, an employee who cooperates with the employer rather than the union representing the employees, or an employee who will not participate in a union strike and continues to work for the employer.

scienter. Literally, a Latin word meaning "knowingly." In law the word has come to mean knowledge, particularly guilty knowledge or knowledge that would establish LIABILITY in civil cases.

scilicet. A Latin word sometimes used in legal documents, meaning "namely" or "that is to say."

scintilla. The smallest trace. The word is sometimes used to mean a mere shred of evidence.

>*Example:* I once had a labor relations case before the famous Judge Learned Hand, who said there was not the proverbial scintilla of evidence that the employer was guilty of an unfair labor practice.

scire facias (SCI. FA.). A common-law WRIT, now abandoned in most states, requiring the person against whom the writ is brought to show cause why the party obtaining the writ should not have the advantage of a court record. (To me as a lawyer the whole proceeding was confusing and does not fit into modern legal practice.)

scope of employment. The field and range of employment. The scope of employment is a term used in WORKMEN'S COMPENSATION lawsuits involving the LIABILITY of employers. The courts in determining the rights of employees have broadened these rights somewhat by asking whether the act of an employee arose out of and occurred during and within the scope of and IN THE COURSE OF his employment.

seal. In ancient days of law a seal was an impression made on wax or a similar substance. A document with a seal was a record which carried great legal effect. Today sealed impressions are seldom made, but instead the initials "L.S." are used, meaning "the place of the seal" (*locum sigilium*).

sealed verdict. Sometimes when a jury reaches its decision, the VERDICT may be placed in an envelope and signed. Later that signed verdict is opened by the judge (generally in the presence of the jury) and announced in court. That is called a sealed verdict.

search and seizure. 1. Search of one's house, office, building, or person by police or other authorities for the purpose of discovering stolen or illegal property or the evidence of criminal guilt. **2.** Forcible seizure of the property or the EVIDENCE found. Our constitutions (state and federal) restrict searches and seizures to those authorized by specifically worded SEARCH WARRANTS.

search warrant. An order authorizing a sheriff or other police official to search premises for property claimed to be illegally held or for evidence of criminal activity. Under state and federal constitutions, such warrants must be carefully and specifically worded.

second mortgage. A MORTGAGE on real estate which is secondary in LIEN to a first mortgage.

secondary boycott. See BOYCOTT.

secondary evidence. When primary, or PRIMA FACIE, EVIDENCE is not available, sometimes evidence may be introduced to prove the contents of an original missing document. Proof of the contents of the original document is then called secondary evidence.

section. 1. In real estate law, a portion of a subdivision. **2.** In some western states, a parcel of land which, according to a government survey, is one square mile (640 acres).

secured creditor. A person who holds or has a LIEN on property of his debtor as security for payment of the debt.

securities. Documents such as STOCKS and BONDS that establish financial claims.

As the result of federal legislation beginning in the 1930s and regulations of the Securities and Exchange Commission (S.E.C.) (established in 1934), there is much law on this subject to protect the investing public. This body of law deals with the promotion and sale of securities and investments, and is intended to control stock market abuses such as those which played a large part in the crash of 1929.

seduction. In general, the act of a man inducing a woman to have sexual intercourse by subtle persuasion, deception, or bribes, without the employment of force. In most states seduction is a crime.

seizin. An ancient term meaning ownership and possession of land, and involving the duty of homage and fealty to a feudal lord. It is a technical term seldom used today.

seizure. Taking possession of property by force.

Selective Service laws. Laws relating to military conscription. Since 1940 a considerable body of law has been built up involving the registration, drafting or deferment, and induction of men for military duty.

self-dealing. The dealing of a trustee or other FIDUCIARY for himself individually in such a way that there is a conflict of interest.

self-defense. An action or the right to protect one's self, one's family, or one's property against attack by another person. It may be a legal justification for assaulting or in some cases killing the attacker.

sentence. In criminal law, a penalty pronounced by a court upon a person who has either pled guilty or been convicted of a crime.

separation. A term most commonly used in marital relations whereby a husband and wife no longer live together as husband and wife, but live separately. Their other marital obligations continue, such as support and obligations having to do with children of the marriage.

sequestration. 1. The seizure or removal of property in order to preserve or conserve it during the course of litigation. Sequestration is an unusual remedy and in some cases is regarded as severe and harsh. **2.** Keeping witnesses out of the courtroom so that they do not hear and cannot be influenced by the testimony of other witnesses. **3.** At the discretion of the trial judge, keeping all the jurors away from the public, or "locking them up," and free from contact with or subject to influence of the PARTIES or the public.

seriatim. A Latin word meaning "separately and serially, one at a time." (I have always felt that it was a poor substitute for the English translation.)

servant. An employee.

serve. In a legal procedure, to hand to or deliver a legal paper to a person.

service. Generally, *personal service* is delivery of a copy of legal PROCESS to a person and leaving it with him. *Substitute service* is any form of service or process other than personal service, such as *service by publication* or *service by mail,* when permitted by law or court order.

session. The period of time when a body, such as a legislative body, a commission, or a judicial tribunal, is sitting or assembled for the transaction of business.

session laws. Bound volumes of proceedings of a particular legislative session.

set-off. In a lawsuit, a counterdemand, independent of the plaintiff's claim, which it may offset. It is to be distinguished from a pure COUNTERCLAIM, which must, according to the statutes in some states, arise out of the same transaction for which the plaintiff sues.

settle out of court. See COMPROMISE AND SETTLEMENT.

settlement. 1. Adjustment, determination, or compromise of an account. **2.** In the case of an ESTATE or a deceased person, the final determination of the rights of beneficiaries of that estate. **3.** See COMPROMISE AND SETTLEMENT.

settlor. A person who creates a TRUST.

sever. To effect a SEVERANCE.

severally. Separately. This adverb is usually used with the word "liable." Persons severally liable are separately liable, and each may be responsible for an entire debt.

severance. This term may apply to both civil and criminal cases. **1.** In a civil case, the word basically means separation. Certain issues, such as the issue of LIABILITY and the issue of DAMAGES, may be tried separately. **2.** In criminal cases, defendants may be tried separately or issues may be separated by severance.

sex discrimination. According to law, male and female persons must be treated equally. As a result, whenever either sex is discriminated against in matters of employment, education, or other activities, charges may be brought on the ground of sex discrimination.

shareholder. See STOCKHOLDER.

Shelley's case, rule in. The famous nineteenth-century American jurist Chancellor James Kent defined the rule in Shelley's case as follows: "Where a person takes an estate of freehold, legally or equitably, under a deed, will, or other writing, and in the same instrument there is a

limitation by way of remainder, either with or without the interposition
of another estate, of any interest of the same legal or equitable quality
to his heirs or heirs of his body, as a class of persons to take in succession from generation to generation, the limitation to the heirs entitles
the ancestor to the whole estate."

That is technicality at its worst. (The *New Yorker* magazine used
to comment on such obscure language by asking: "Any questions?")
A smart aleck taking a bar examination was asked to state the "Rule
in Shelley's case." He quipped, "The rule in Shelley's case is the
same as in any other person's case. The law is no respecter of persons."

sheriff. The chief executive officer of a county's law enforcement agency,
having both civil and criminal duties. A sheriff is usually elected by the
people. Sheriffs and their deputies are peace officers and enforce criminal laws. Generally a sheriff must also serve all processes and legal
papers turned over to him for that purpose.

Sherman Antitrust Act. A law passed by Congress in 1890 which provides
that there shall be no contracts, combinations, or conspiracies in restraint of trade affecting INTERSTATE COMMERCE. See COMBINATION IN
RESTRAINT OF TRADE and MONOPOLY.

shifting the burden of proof. In general it is the plaintiff who is obligated to
prove certain facts in a court of law—who has the BURDEN OF PROOF.
But often additional EVIDENCE may place that burden on another party
to the lawsuit. That is called shifting the burden of proof.

shopbook rule. A generally accepted rule of EVIDENCE to the effect that any
writing, book of record, or document made or kept in the regular course
of business is admissible in evidence in a court trial.

short selling. Generally, the sale of corporate STOCK by a person who does
not own the stock but who expects to buy it when the price is lower.

show cause order. An order of the court granted on the application of a
party to litigation requiring the adverse party to show cause on a certain date why certain judicial relief should not be granted; sometimes
called a "short notice of motion."

shyster. A disreputable lawyer.

sine die. A Latin phrase meaning "without a day." When a deliberative
body concludes its business and makes a final adjournment without setting a date for the next meeting, that is an adjournment *sine die.*

sine qua non. That which is necessary or indispensable. From the Latin
"without which not."

sinecure. Employment, public or private, in which the employee is paid but
has relatively few duties.

situate. Located or having a fixed position.

situs. A Latin word often used in law meaning the place where a thing or
person is located.

slander. Oral DEFAMATION of a person, as distinguished from libel, which is written.

> *Example:* John Doe thoroughly dislikes Richard Roe, a lawyer. In business circles and at lunches, Doe says that Roe is not competent as a lawyer and is a thief. Doe is guilty of slander.

See LIBEL AND SLANDER.

smart money. Another term for *punitive damages*. See DAMAGES.

smoking gun. A slang expression indicating that circumstantial evidence points to the guilt of the accused.

sodomy. "Unnatural" sexual intercourse.

solely. A word of limits or restriction. Of course it means alone, but in law it is used mostly frequently as meaning *exclusively*.

solicitor. In English law, an ATTORNEY who is an office lawyer or whose practice is limited to courts of EQUITY. See BARRISTER.

solicitor general. An attorney who is an officer of a federal or state department of justice, and who presents cases for the government in the highest courts.

sound mind. The mental faculties of a person whose mentality is not impaired. It is often used in the case of a person who makes a will or contract.

sovereign immunity. An ancient doctrine (*"the king can do no wrong"*) that provides that a government cannot be sued. Many states today have abolished this rule. See IMMUNITY and FEDERAL TORT CLAIMS ACT.

special. Something not regular or something particular, such as a *special meeting* or a *special term of court*.

specialist. In the practice of law, a person who has given special study to or who specializes in one particular branch of the law.

> *Example:* Some law schools have special courses in the field of taxation and grant master's degrees in taxation to students who complete the extra course in taxation. Lawyers who receive the degree of Master of Taxation often become specialists in taxation.

specific performance. Whenever a contract is broken, the normal legal REMEDY is an action for money DAMAGES for the BREACH OF CONTRACT. There are, however, many cases where the remedy of money damages is an inadequate remedy, and in such cases the court may compel the performance of the contract by the parties. This remedy is called specific performance.

specifications. A statement of details, such as those attached to the CONTRACT prepared by an architect outlining particulars of the building to be erected.

speculate. To think about, often in a casual way. It is guesswork about facts and a person's arrival at a conclusion by unproven assumption.

speech, freedom of. See CONSTITUTIONAL LAW.

spendthrift trust. A TRUST created to provide a fund to MAINTAIN a BENEFI-CIARY and at the same time to secure that trust against the beneficiary's improvidence. The document setting up the trust often provides that the beneficiary cannot transfer the fund or property or assign any interest to his creditors.

squatter. A person who lives on land of another without any legal right or permission. A squatter uses the land as if he owned it, though he does not in fact have any legal interest in it. See ADVERSE POSSESSION.

stale. A term used in law to describe something that once was but no longer is effective.

> *Example:* According to the laws of many states, a bank is not required to honor a check if it is dated 6 months before it is delivered to the bank. Such a check is a stale check.

stare decisis. A Latin phrase ("to stand by the decided") meaning that courts should follow the principles set forth in previously decided court cases.

state (v.). To express something in writing; to declare or allege a fact or series of facts.

state (n.). **1.** A body of people permanently established within certain geographical limits and whose government exercises sovereign jurisdiction over or within this territory. **2.** One of the 50 states of the United States. **3.** The public, a term used in criminal trials (*"The State* v. *John Doe"*).

state's evidence. The EVIDENCE a participant in a crime gives incriminating others while admitting his own participation in the crime. The person turning state's evidence generally does so in the expectation of a pardon or a light sentence.

status quo. A condition or situation in which a person or thing is; the existing situation. The *status quo ante* is the situation as it was before a particular event.

statute. A law passed by a legislature.

statute of frauds. A law adopted by most states requiring that certain contracts and causes of action be in writing and signed by the persons to be obligated by the contract.

statute of limitations. A law stating the time within which an action or court proceeding must be brought. See LIMITATIONS OF ACTIONS.

statutory. 1. Relating to a statute. **2.** Created or regulated by statute.

statutory rape. See RAPE.

stay (n.). A restraining order or INJUNCTION.

stay (v.). To stop, hold back, check, or postpone.

stipulation. An agreement between attorneys, generally written and signed by the attorneys, which may be produced before a court in connection with a legal proceeding.

stock. 1. In agricultural law, domestic animals. **2.** In mercantile circles it

means goods, wares, and merchandise used in trade. **3.** In the CORPO-
RATION world, (a) money invested in a business and (b) the capital of a
corporation raised by the sale of shares of stock. A share of stock is a
fractional INTEREST of a STOCKHOLDER in the ownership of a corporation.

stockholder. A person who owns corporate stock. Corporate stock evidences
the ownership of a corporation. That means that the body of stockholders in a corporation are in effect its owners. Also called *shareholder.*

straight-line depreciation. A method used in ACCOUNTING whereby the
original cost of an asset such as property is divided into that number
of years in which the asset is expected to remain in service, arriving
at a reasonable constant fraction of that cost as the annual depreciation.

strictum jus. A Latin phrase that literally means "by strict law"; hence, by
the letter of the law.

strike. In LABOR RELATIONS LAW, a cessation of work by employees in an
attempt to compel an employer to grant their demands. This is a tool
labor can use against management. Strikes, which were illegal until the
midnineteenth century, are now recognized as valid in the private sec-
tor, although they are usually prohibited to government employees.

strikebreaker. A person hired by an employer to take the place of an employee on STRIKE. A strikebreaker is different from a SCAB, who was an
employee before the strike was called and continues to work during it.

striking a jury. In some parts of the country, the process of selecting a
PETIT JURY to serve on the trial of a case. In other areas the procedure
is simply called selecting a JURY.

sua sponte. Latin for "of his own will." When a judge or a court takes
some action without prompting on the part of a lawyer, the judge or
court is said to act *sua sponte.*

subcontractor. When a principal contractor makes another person responsible for part of the work specified in the principal contractor's contract,
that second person is called a subcontractor.

subdivision. See POLITICAL SUBDIVISION.

subjective symptoms. In personal INJURY law cases, medical symptoms are
either subjective or objective. Subjective symptoms, such as headaches
and nausea, are those evidenced only by statements made by the patient; *objective symptoms* are those which, like broken bones, can be
determined by a physician, irrespective of what the patient tells the
physician.

submission of controversy. A consent proceeding: that is, a substitute for an
ACTION, such as agreement to accept the decision of ARBITRATION, allowed by certain states. Whether or not a controversy may be *submitted* depends on the statutes of a particular state.

subornation of perjury. The crime of persuading or bribing another person to commit perjury.

subpoena. A PROCESS requiring a person to attend a trial or hearing and testify as a witness. A *subpoena duces tecum* (Latin, "bring with you") is a subpoena requiring a witness to produce some specified book, object, or paper in court.

subrogation. When a person pays a debt or claim for which another person is liable, he may be substituted for the original creditor and have the right to collect from the debtor. That is called subrogation.

> *Example:* Excelsior Fire Insurance Company insured John Jones' hotel for loss occasioned by fire. The hotel was partially destroyed by a fire caused by a contractor's use of a blowtorch. The Excelsior Fire Insurance Company paid Jones for his loss and thereby became *subrogated* to Jones' claim against the contractor for his negligence in setting fire to the hotel; the contractor was now liable to Excelsior rather than Jones.

See SUBROGEE.

subrogee. A person to whom rights are subrogated: that is, a person who succeeds to the rights of another by reason of SUBROGATION.

subscribe. In general, to sign one's name at the end of a document. A person who signs his name to a document subscribes to that document, thereby accepting it.

subscribing witness. A person who witnesses the signing of a document by another person and attests this signing by signing the document himself.

subscription. 1. Signing one's name at the end of a document. **2.** An agreement or contract to contribute money for a particular purpose.

subsidiary. When a PARENT CORPORATION or HOLDING COMPANY owns or controls another corporation, the corporation it owns or controls is called a subsidiary.

substantial. Considerable; large. Substantial is not an exact word; it may mean different things to different people. The use of the term in legal documents may result in misunderstandings.

> *Example:* I once had a court case involving cancellation of a lease. The lease said that either party could cancel it in the event of substantial damage by fire to the leased premises. The court held that the landlord could not cancel the lease because the phrase "substantial damage" was too vague and indefinite.

substantive law. Law that defines and regulates the rights and obligations of individual persons and determines whether a litigant has a right to sue. It is to be distinguished from *adjective,* or *procedural,* law, which governs practice and procedure.

subtenant. A person who rents some or a portion of leased property from a tenant.

succession. The passing of TITLE to property under the laws of DESCENT AND DISTRIBUTION.

sui generis. Latin, "of its own kind"; the definition has been extended to mean the only one of its kind.

sui juris. Competent; legally capable of managing one's own affairs. See NON SUI JURIS.

suit. A lawsuit. An ACTION in court. A suit may also be a legal PROCEEDING that is not an action.

summary. Short and brief. A *summary proceeding* seeks to avoid undue legal delays.

summation (summing up). Presentation to a jury of the final arguments in a case by a lawyer for either side. Each lawyer summarizes the EVIDENCE and presents points designed to convince the jury to render a favorable VERDICT.

summons. A legal WRIT or PROCESS requiring a defendant to answer a COMPLAINT in a lawsuit or otherwise appear in the case. See CITATION.

sunshine laws. The name popularly given to laws which require government or public agencies to make their meetings open to the public, or to make public the information discussed at said meetings.

superior court. See COURT.

supersedeas. A court order commanding the STAY of some legal proceeding. (Latin, "you shall refrain.")

supra. A Latin word meaning "above"; in legal writing it means that which precedes the material the reader is reading. See INFRA.

supreme. The highest. Hence in the federal government and most state governments (except New York—see COURT), courts having the last word in matters of law are usually called supreme courts. The U.S. Constitution is called the "supreme law of the land."

suretyship. A contract whereby one person undertakes to perform legal obligations of another.

surrender. Generally, giving up, as of real estate.

> *Example:* John Jones leases a parcel of real estate to Sam Smith for a term of two years. After a year, Jones is sorry he leased the property to Smith and persuades Smith to surrender the leased premises.

surrogate. In most American states, the title given to the judge who is in charge of the estates of deceased persons. See ORDINARY.

suspended sentence. Punishment for a crime that is withheld by the court upon certain conditions. See PROBATION and REPRIEVE.

swear. To take a solemn oath with an appeal to God, usually with one hand on the Bible. In some states in lieu of an oath a witness is permitted to make a solemn declaration as to the truth of testimony or a statement.

167 **syndicate**

This is called an *affirmation*, and is used for people whose religions prohibit the use of the deity's name or who do not believe in the Judeo-Christian deity.

sweatshop. A place where employees are underpaid and overworked or exploited under very bad physical conditions.

swindle. To cheat or defraud.

syndicate. In business law, a group of individuals or organizations formed for the purpose of conducting and carrying out some business enterprise.

T

talesman. 1. A bystander who is summoned by the court to act as a juror when the usual panel of jurors has been exhausted. **2.** A member of a pool from which jurors are selected.

tariff. A duty imposed upon property imported into the United States. Sometimes the schedule of items subject to duty and the rates at which they are taxed is also called a tariff.

tax. An amount imposed by the government on ownership, transfer, or sale of property, or on income earned by citizens, or on devolution of inheritance or gifts of property.

tax avoidance. See TAX EVASION.

Tax Court of the United States. A court with jurisdiction over federal tax cases.

tax deed. A conveyance of real estate made by a unit of government as a result of a sale of lands for nonpayment of taxes. Tax deeds are very common; but they are often not given great weight by real estate title experts, because frequently a defect can be proven in the proceedings leading up to the TAX SALE.

tax evasion. There are two terms that are commonly misused: tax evasion and *tax avoidance*. Tax evasion is illegal and improper, because it involves an element of fraud and deceit. Tax avoidance is legal, because it is the result of taking legitimate steps or proceedings that lead to avoiding the imposition of a tax.

tax sale. Sale of REAL ESTATE by a governmental agency for the nonpayment of taxes.

taxable year. A phrase used in INCOME TAX law to indicate a tax ACCOUNT-
ING period. In other words, some taxpayers account for their income on
the basis of a calendar year—January 1 to December 31; other taxpayers may do so on the basis of a *fiscal year* that differs from the calendar year—May 1 to April 30, for example.

tenancy. The interest a person has in REAL ESTATE. It may be a JOINT
TENANCY; a TENANCY IN COMMON; a tenancy from month to month or
from year to year; a TENANCY AT WILL; or a tenancy for a certain
number of years.

tenancy at will. Occupation of real estate by a tenant without a written
lease and without agreement for a definite term. It may be terminated
by landlord or tenant at will.

tenancy by the entirety. See ENTIRETY.

tenancy in common. An arrangement whereby people each own a separate
fractional INTEREST in property and are each entitled to possession of
the property. A *tenant in common* may sell or assign his interest in the
property without the consent of the other tenants.

tenant. See LEASE.

tender. In legal matters, an offer to pay money or perform a contract.
Tender presupposes ability to perform on the part of the person who
makes the tender. Sometimes, in the case of tendering money, a tender
must be guaranteed by paying the money into court.

tenement. Real property in which a tenant has a semipermanent interest. In
common use, a tenement is a multifamily dwelling house often occupied
by poor people and maintained in a shabby to UNTENANTABLE condition.

tenure. A term that refers to the manner or means or conditions under
which real property is held. Sometimes it may refer to conditions or
terms under which an office or government position is held. In common
use, a teacher or professor receives tenure, or the right to continue his
or her employment for a term of years or until retirement, upon com-
pletion of a prior probationary period and/or certain scholarly pursuits.

term. In legal terminology, a particular session of court.

Example: John Doe sues Richard Roe. The case will be tried at the
October term of court.

testament. See WILL.

testamentary. Having to do with a WILL.

Example: John Smith makes a will giving the sum of $25,000 to his
friend, Tom Brown, as trustee, to hold in trust for the benefit of
Smith's son. Smith has created a *testamentary trust.*

testator (testatrix). A person who makes a WILL.

testify. To give EVIDENCE under OATH in a court of law or other hearing.

testimony. Generally, oral EVIDENCE given under OATH by a WITNESS in court or at a hearing.

theft. The act of stealing money or property.

third party. An outsider with no direct interest in a transaction.

third-party beneficiary. A person who is not a party to a contract but who benefits from the contract and may enforce rights under it.

> *Example:* John Doe enters into a contract with Herbert Smith whereby Smith agrees to rent a designated house and lot to Jones's son for a three-year period. Jones's son may enforce the contract against Smith as a third-party beneficiary.

title. In real estate law, ownership of REAL ESTATE.

toll. An amount paid for the use of a bridge, road, ferry, or something else of a public nature.

tort. The legal word for a wrongful, unlawful civil act other than a BREACH OF CONTRACT. There are many torts, including NEGLIGENCE, NUISANCE, LIBEL AND SLANDER, ASSAULT AND BATTERY, and almost any other infringement of another person's rights.

tort-feasor. Basically, a wrongdoer; a person who commits a TORT.

tortious. Wrongful, unlawful, involving TORT.

Totten trust. The deposit of money in a bank by one person in his own name as trustee for another.

towage. In ADMIRALTY LAW, towing or pulling one vessel by another vessel. Generally towage is applied to increase the speed of the vessel towed, and the towing is done by a tugboat. The price paid for the towing is also called towage. There are special rules of law governing tugs and towees.

town. A unit of government smaller than a city and larger than a village; in some states it is a division of a county.

trade acceptance. A bill of exchange or draft drawn by a seller on a buyer. (A term rarely used in commercial practice.)

trademark. A mark, name, or symbol usually attached to goods sold in the open market to identify the goods sold and the manufacturer and/or seller of the goods. It may not be used by others. The purpose of a trademark is to prevent trading on the goodwill of another party and to avoid confusion. (It has become difficult in many cases to prevent trademarks from turning into generic names: In every day speech people refer to any paper handkerchief as a Kleenex, and to any photocopier as a Xerox machine, though this may be inaccurate.) Whether a trademark is registered under federal or a state statute depends on the area where a product is to be marketed. If it is marketed only within one state, then state registration may be sufficient. If the product is sold in interstate commerce, then registration with the Federal Patent Office is desirable.

trading stamps. Stamps, the number of which is dependent upon the amount of the purchase, given by a merchant to his customers entitling them to receive goods in exchange for a certain number of stamps. There are three parties to the transaction: (a) the merchant, who buys the stamps from the trading stamp company; (b) the trading stamp company, which supplies the exchange goods; and (c) the customer, who gets the stamps when he buys from the merchant. Trading stamp procedures are subject to government regulations and control.

transcript. 1. A written, typed, or printed copy of legal proceedings. **2.** An official copy of a legal document or record.

transfer. To convey or remove property from one place or person to another.

transferee. The person to whom a transfer is made. A *transferor* is the person who makes the transfer.

trauma. A wound or BODILY INJURY caused by physical violence or stress. The word is more apt to be a medical than a legal term, but is often used in a legal connection.

traverse. In a legal sense, to deny allegations of facts presented in a legal PLEADING.

treason. An attempt by overt acts to overthrow the government of one's country, or the giving of aid and comfort to an enemy of one's country. According to the U.S. Constitution, "No persons shall be convicted of treason unless on the testimony of two witnesses to the same overt act, or on confession in open court" (Article III, Section 3).

treasury stock. The stock of a corporation originally fully paid for and transferred to a STOCKHOLDER, which is subsequently reacquired by the corporation.

treaty. A written and formally signed contract between two or more nations.

treble damages. A penalty allowed by some statutes whereby a defendant is obliged to pay three times the amount of DAMAGES found by a jury.

> *Example:* John Jones owned a small tract of timber. Richard Roe wrongfully and maliciously cut many trees in the timber tract. A jury found that the cut trees were worth $800. In the state where the parties lived, a person who willfully cuts the trees of another person is liable for treble damages. Hence $2,400 was ordered by the court against Roe for treble damages.

trespass. Fundamentally, the doing of an unlawful act, or of a lawful act in an unlawful manner, to the INJURY of another's person or property. The most common use of the term refers to breaking into or entering upon another person's real property. Technically, every unauthorized entry on another's real property is trespass, although DAMAGES for mere entering may be hard to prove. Every trespass gives the owner of that real property a right to at least nominal damages.

trial. The examination of the facts of a case by a judicial TRIBUNAL, and a determination of the right and wrong of the case or the guilt or innocence of a DEFENDANT. A trial has a number of parts. It is a vital element of a legal proceeding.

Preliminary steps include propounding of INTERROGATORIES, DISCOVERY proceedings, and MOTIONS of all sorts. When preliminaries are completed, the case has to be brought to trial, and often there are pretrial conferences with the judge who will preside at the trial. The case is then placed on a DOCKET, and cases are called for trial in numerical order. In the ordinary case bystanders and interested persons as well as parties to the case are permitted to attend the trial. A *court reporter*—sometimes a stenotypist—takes minutes of the trial and makes a record of all that is said and done.

EVIDENCE is introduced first by the PLAINTIFF or the PROSECUTOR in civil and criminal cases respectively, and then the lawyer for the defendant makes CROSS-EXAMINATION of the plaintiff's or prosecutor's witnesses. Then the defendant produces evidence, and the lawyer for the plaintiff or the prosecutor cross-examines the defendant's witnesses. After all evidence is introduced by both sides, the "evidence is closed," and various motions are made by the lawyers for both sides for directed verdicts or other RELIEF. Then both lawyers make their final arguments—summations—to the jury, and the judge gives INSTRUCTION to the jury as to the law applicable to the case. The jury deliberates and finally agrees upon a VERDICT (or, if it cannot agree, announces a HUNG JURY).

If the case is heard by a judge without a jury, much of the same procedure is followed except that there are no summations or instructions to a jury. In place of summations the court may require the lawyers to file BRIEFS.

tribunal. A COURT or other body that decides legal matters. Every court is a tribunal, but some tribunals lack some of the powers and authority of a court.

trover. A common-law action to recover DAMAGES for wrongful conversion of personal property.

true bill. An indorsement made by a GRAND JURY or an INDICTMENT when it returns that indictment against a person accused of a crime (in other words, when it finds that a crime has been committed and there is reason to believe the accused committed it).

trust. Legal title to property held by one person (the *trustee*) for another. The BENEFICIARY of a trust is called the *cestui qui trust*.

The *trustor* (also called the *donor* or *creator*) is the person who creates or establishes a trust, either by will or a trust agreement.

When a trustee accepts a trust, he is bound to administer it in accordance with its terms. If he violates a trust, he is guilty of a BREACH OF TRUST and is liable to the beneficiary for any loss. A trustee owes to a beneficiary a high degree of CARE and must act not for his own personal advantage but for the best interests of the beneficiary. The law says that a trustee must not use the trust property for his own benefit or profit to the detriment of the beneficiary or beneficiaries. In other words, the trustee must not use the trust property for his own interest, and must avoid any conflict with the interests of the beneficiaries. He is prohibited by law from acquiring any interest adverse to the trust or the beneficiaries. All in all, holding a trust is a ticklish job. A trustee must walk a narrow path, and must perserve and protect the trust property from any waste or loss. He must be prepared to account to the beneficiaries for every nickel or dime that comes into his POSSESSION. A trustee is authorized to be compensated for performing his duties as a trustee at a rate or commission fixed by the law of the particular state.

trust deed. See MORTGAGE.

trust *ex maleficio*. A trust that arises out of someone's wrongdoing. When a person acquires property, a court of EQUITY may find that a trust should be implied, with the wrongdoer responsible as a trustee would be.

> *Example.* John Doe sends Richard Roe as his agent to an auction sale to buy a piece of real estate. Richard Roe buys the piece of property in his own name rather than as agent for John Doe. John Doe brings an action against Richard Roe, asking the court to rule that Richard Roe holds the property as trustee *ex maleficio* for the benefit of John Doe. The court finds in favor of John Doe and rules that Richard Roe holds the property as agent or trustee for John Doe.

trustee. See TRUST.

try. To hold a trial or bring a person to trial.

U

ultra vires. Beyond the power, CAPACITY, or authority. A Latin phrase used in law principally in connection with corporations.

> *Example:* I once represented an advertising corporation, which we will call the Jones Corporation, that bought a radio station. The purchase had to be approved by the Federal Communications Commission (F.C.C.). The F.C.C. would not approve the new ownership of the radio station by the Jones Corporation because such ownership would be *ultra vires,* that is, beyond the power of the corporation, which was chartered as an advertising company. The F.C.C. required us to amend the charter of the Jones Corporation so that it had power to own and operate a radio station before the purchase could be approved.

unclean hands. See CLEAN HANDS.

unconscionable. Contrary to good conscience or shockingly inequitable. A word frequently used in law cases.

unconstitutional. In law, a term used to designate an action or law in conflict with the United States Constitution or the constitution of some state. See CONSTITUTIONAL LAW.

undersheriff. A deputy SHERIFF, perhaps a sheriff's chief DEPUTY, who acts directly under orders of the sheriff or takes over for him if he dies or becomes incapacitated.

undersigned. The person or persons whose name or names are signed at the end of a document. See SUBSCRIBE.

undertaking. A written document given as security for the performance of some act or for something required in a legal proceeding.

underwrite. In business law, to guarantee the sale price of corporate securities such as stocks or bonds.

undisclosed principal. A party represented by an AGENT who does not give notice to another party that he is acting for a principal.

undivided profits. A term used in ACCOUNTING documents to mean profits of a CORPORATION which have not been paid out as DIVIDENDS to STOCKHOLDERS.

undue influence. Influence that is improperly exercised on a person so as to prevent him from freely exercising his own will.

> *Example:* Mary Jane Smith has a lifelong friend, a distant relative named Barbara Jones, whom she invites to live with her. Smith is in poor health and is senile. She is very dependent on Jones, to the extent that she cuts off all relationship with her own children. Jones persuades Smith to execute a will giving Jones the bulk of her estate. When Smith dies, her children contest the will. The WILL CONTEST case is tried before a jury that determines that Smith was subject to undue influence by Jones.

unethical. Obviously, referring to that which is not ethical.

unfair. A characterization frequently used by organized labor to refer to labor practices of an employer, and less frequently by employers to refer to labor activities. See LABOR RELATIONS LAWS.

unfair competition. A term used in trade relations to indicate tactics used by a competitor that are dishonest or fraudulent.

uniform state laws. Model laws drafted by an organization known as the National Conference of Commissioners on Uniform State Laws, which has attempted over the years to establish some uniformity in state laws. It is a difficult task, because each state is of course independent of other states. The Conference has, however, been successful in having many of its model laws enacted.

unilateral. One-sided. In law as applied to a contract or transaction, the acts or obligations of only one of the two or more persons to such contract or transaction are unilateral.

union shop. In labor relations law, an establishment in which all workers must be members of the union, either prior to or upon employment. Compare CLOSED SHOP and OPEN SHOP.

United States marshal. An officer of a United States District Court with duties comparable to the duties of a SHERIFF in state courts. United States marshals are appointed by the president of the United States.

unjust enrichment. A doctrine in law and EQUITY that says that a person may not profit inequitably at another's expense.

unlawful assembly. A meeting of a number of persons to pursue an unlawful plan that seems likely to disturb the peace.

unliquidated. Referring to that which has not been determined or made certain. See LIQUIDATED.

unmarketable title. The title to real estate offered to a prospective purchaser when there are certain title defects which would probably subject him to vexatious litigation.

unreasonable restraint of trade. See RESTRAINT OF TRADE.

unsound mind. An infirmity of mind that renders a person incapable of managing himself or his affairs. The phrase—or its Latin version, *non compos mentis*—is often used in cases contesting the validity of wills or contracts, and indicates that the persons in question are incapable of validly making such documents. See SOUND MIND.

untenantable. A word frequently used in landlord-tenant law to mean the condition of leased premises that are not fit for occupancy or rental.

unwritten law. Law may be *written* or *unwritten*. Written law generally is found in statutes or ordinances, whereas unwritten law is generally statements of principles found in court decisions or common law. This phrase is sometimes used to refer to a mythical, nonlegal rule of law that says a man may take the life of his wife's lover with impunity.

usage. A custom so well established that it may be presumed to be generally understood and thus, for example, be an implied part of a contract.

use. The right of a beneficiary to the profits and benefits of land and property.

usufruct. The earnings or profits of property, or the right to use and enjoy property of another.

usurp. To seize or hold any office or position without legal right. The term may also apply to the unlawful seizure of places and powers.

usury. Charging or contracting for interest on a money loan at a rate in excess of the amount allowed by law. Some state laws provide that a creditor cannot collect the amount of money lent a debtor if the interest charged is *usurious*.

V

v. (vs.) An abbreviation for the word "versus," meaning against.

> *Example:* John Jones sues Howard Smith. The case is known as "John Jones versus Howard Smith." The abbreviation for the title of the case is *Jones* v. *Smith*.

vacate. 1. To set aside or make void. 2. To ABANDON real property.

vagrancy. A term that includes idleness, unemployment, and the condition of having no visible means of support. The United States Supreme Court has held certain state statutes prohibiting vagrancy as being too vague and indefinite.

valid. Having legal force; legally sound or binding, such as a valid contract.

validate. To make valid.

valuable consideration. That CONSIDERATION which will support a contract. Valuable consideration does not have to be expressed in dollars and cents; it may be a promise or a benefit accruing to one party or some forbearance or detriment to another party.

value received. The amount of lawful CONSIDERATION received in exchange for a contract or a negotiable instrument.

vein. In MINING LAW, a bed of mineral in the ground or in a mountain, separated from and distinguishable from neighboring rock or earth.

vendee. A buyer or purchaser of real property.

vendor. A seller of real property.

venireman. A member of a *venire,* or panel, from which jurors are chosen.

venue. The place of trial of an action or legal proceeding. See CHANGE OF VENUE.

veracity. Truthfulness. In most cases a judge or jury may be called upon to evaluate the veracity of witnesses. See CREDIBILITY.

verdict. A word derived from the Latin "true saying." Usually in law a verdict is the decision of a jury on questions of fact submitted to it.

verification. In legal proceedings, a sworn, written statement that something such as a document is true.

vested. In the law of property, fixed, settled, or absolute (e.g., an established interest in property that cannot be taken away by any subsequent events).

veto. A word (from the Latin "I forbid") meaning the refusal by an executive officer (a governor of a state or the president of the United States), or in the case of the United Nations by a member country, to approve a law passed by a legislature or other body. Congress and the state legislatures may override an executive veto in most cases by a two-thirds vote.

vires. See ULTRA VIRES.

vital statistics. Public records relating to the birth, marriage, and death of persons. These records are kept by a branch of government, such as a city department of health.

viva voce. By voice or orally; aloud.

> ***Example:*** An examination of a witness may be *viva voce* (orally) or by written INTERROGATORY.

void. Of no legal force or effect.

voidable. Susceptible of being made VOID; referring to something that may be set aside or annulled.

voir dire. The interrogation of a member of a panel of prospective jurors to determine his or her fitness to serve.

voting trust. A TRUST established by stockholders of a CORPORATION whereby they authorize a person who serves as a trustee to vote their STOCK.

W

Wagner Act. See LABOR RELATIONS LAWS.

waiver. Basically, the intentional giving up of some right, advantage, or benefit. In law there are many kinds of waivers.

wanton. In the law of NEGLIGENCE, a term frequently used to describe that which is reckless or malicious, or flagrantly disregards the rights of other people, as *wanton neglect*.

ward. A person for whom a GUARDIAN is appointed. Ordinarily a ward is either a MINOR or a person under some legal DISABILITY, such as an INCOMPETENT.

warehouseman. A person engaged in the business of receiving and storing goods for other people.

warrant. Written authorization. In criminal law, a *warrant for arrest* is a written command of a court directed to an officer to arrest a person and bring him before a court. Other warrants in criminal proceedings include a warrant for commitment issued after sentence, a SEARCH WARRANT, and a warrant for EXTRADITION.

warranty. A promise or guarantee that certain facts are true. Warranties play an important part in the law of insurance and the law of sales. In insurance law, warranties are promises by an insured that certain relevant facts are true. In sales of personal property, warranties are promises by the seller as to the title and quality of goods. Promises in the case of sales of goods may be *express* or *implied*.

warranty deed. See BREACH OF WARRANTY and DEED.

waste. In the law of real property, any unlawful act by a person in possession of real property that causes INJURY to or destruction of that property.

wear and tear. A phrase often used in the law of leases to mean DEPRECI-ATION as the result of reasonable use over a period of time.

weight of evidence. The greater amount of believable EVIDENCE offered at a trial in support of one side or the other. See PREPONDERANCE.

whereas. A word used as an introduction to a paragraph in a contract or a resolution to mean "in view of the fact that." It is the mark of a legal instrument prepared by a lawyer.

Whiteacre. See BLACKACRE.

wholly and permanently disabled. A term used in insurance to refer to a person who because of his physical condition is incapacitated to work at his usual vocation. See DISABILITY.

will. A statement made by a person of what he wants done with his property after his death. Another word for will is *testament.* Sometimes the words "will" and "testament" are, though redundantly, used together, as "will and testament." A person who makes a will must be of SOUND MIND and free from DISABILITY such as insanity, severe illness, or loss of memory.

A will has to be executed with certain formalities specified by the laws of the state where the will is executed. A will may be attacked because of FRAUD, MISTAKE, or UNDUE INFLUENCE.

Although many years may elapse between the making of a will and the death of a TESTATOR (the person making the will), the will speaks as of the date of death of the testator. In order for a will to have any legal effect, it must be *probated* (proved in court), and notice of PROBATE must be given to any person who or whose property interest would be adversely affected by the probate.

After the will is probated, it may be subject to a *construction pro-ceeding;* that is, the meaning of certain words or phrases in the will may have to be judicially interpreted to determine the true INTENT of the testator. Language used in a will is supposed to be clear and simple, but you would be surprised how complicated it can be.

There are different kinds of wills, including the *statutory will* (executed with all the formalities prescribed by statute); the *holographic will* (handwritten, dated, and signed by the testator); the *joint will* (made by two or more persons and signed by both or all of them—joint wills are seldom used, and are disapproved of by most authorities); and *mutual wills* (separate documents executed by two or more persons in which they make reciprocal provisions for the benefit of the other or others).

will contest. A legal proceeding for the purpose of determining whether or not a WILL in question is the free will of the testator; whether it was legally executed; in other words, whether it is a valid will.

willful. Intentional and voluntary as distinguished from accidental.

willful and malicious injury. An INJURY intentionally inflicted by one person upon another.

wind up. To LIQUIDATE a business (generally a CORPORATION) by collecting assets, paying creditors, and distributing the balance, if any, to STOCKHOLDERS or owners.

with prejudice; without prejudice. 1. Whenever an action is dismissed, there is a statement that it is dismissed either *with prejudice* or *without prejudice*. If the court action is dismissed with prejudice, it means that the action involved is completely dismissed as though that action had been prosecuted to a complete conclusion. If the action is dismissed without prejudice, it means that a new action for the same REMEDY may be instituted. See DISMISS. **2.** If an offer of settlement is made without prejudice, it means that it is not an admission of liability.

without recourse. A phrase used in indorsing a negotiable instrument; it means that the indorser simply transfers title, with notification to future owners of the instrument that the indorser shall not be liable for payment. See QUALIFIED INDORSEMENT.

witness. 1. A person who sees an act or event; in other words, a beholder or spectator. **2.** One who testifies under oath in a court of law. Sometimes a witness may be both a spectator and one who testifies in court as to what he has seen as a spectator.

women's suffrage. See ELECTION.

word of art. A word which, when used in connection with a science or profession, has a particular meaning that differs from the ordinary or dictionary meaning.

work product. The result of work done by an attorney in connection with a lawsuit. Generally a work product is confidential and may not be disclosed to an adversary.

workmen's compensation. A system that provides benefits to employees injured or otherwise disabled IN THE COURSE OF their employment. The unique feature of workmen's compensation is that benefits are payable irrespective of whether the employee, the employer, or others are to blame for an accident. Workmen's compensation is based on state legislation and is funded by means of insurance for which employers pay.

In some states the word "workmen's" has been changed to "workers'."

writ. Generally, a court order addressed to an officer of the law directing him to perform certain acts.

writ of error. An old common-law term referring to an order of an appellate court requiring the trial court to send up the record of the trial for review.

writ of execution. A court order requiring a sheriff to levy on a judgment debtor's property, and to sell that property to satisfy a judgment. Today in most states a simple EXECUTION directed to a sheriff to take similar action is now used in place of a writ of execution.

wrong. A violation of the rights of others. Generally it involves an INJURY to the person, property, or rights of another person.

wrongdoer. A person who violates the rights of another person or persons.

wrongful death statute. The law of a particular state, as passed by its legislature, giving the executor, administrator, or heirs of a deceased person a CAUSE OF ACTION for injuries to the deceased that resulted from the wrongful act or acts of another. In the absence of such a statute, there is no common-law cause of action for wrongful death.

Y

yellow-dog contract. A term of opprobrium used by trade unions to designate a contract that an employee signs promising his employer that he will not join a labor union during his employment. See LABOR RELATIONS LAWS.

yield (v.). As used in the law of property or in connection with legal rights, to surrender or give up.

yield (n.). Net return on investment.

Z

zoning. A system of legislation that divides certain portions of municipalities into districts and regulates building construction and land use in those districts. Much law has been developed over the years with reference to the validity of zoning regulations and their construction, amendment, and enforcement.